Dark Clouds over Europe

The latent danger of renewed tyranny?

Dark Clouds over Europe

The latent danger of renewed tyranny?

by Theodor Abt

Translated by David Roscoe

LIVING HUMAN HERITAGE PUBLICATIONS, ZURICH
2014

Living Human Heritage Publications
Münsterhof 16, 8001 Zurich, Switzerland
Frontispiece: © swa182
info@livinghumanheritage.org
www.livinghumanheritage.org

ISBN-13 978-3-9523880-8-2

LAYOUT: Merve Çakıroğlu and Theodor Abt

PRINTING AND BINDING:
MAS MATBAACILIK A.Ş.
Hamidiye Mahallesi Soğuksu Caddesi
No:3 34408 Kağıthane, İstanbul / Türkiye
T. +90 212 294 10 00 (pbx) F. +90 212 294 90 80
info@masmat.com.tr

List of contents

Acknowledgements

This work would never have been embarked on had it not been for the moral support and caring guidance of Dr. Marie-Louise von Franz (1915-1998). That was in the early 90s. Thanks to her far-sightedness, she was able to recognise much more clearly than I the significance of the dreams about the situation in Switzerland that I had collected at that time. Her many pointers with regard to their interpretation enabled me to gain an overall picture of the various dreams presented here.

For the initial processing and updating of the work at that time, my thanks go to various friends and acquaintances. I cannot list them individually, but I should like to express my thanks to all of them. I should also like to thank all those who shared with me their dreams about federal independence or about our future in general, and allowed me to use them for my observations.

Special thanks go to my dear wife Regina Abt-Baechi and our two daughters, Sabine and Doris, for constantly reviving my flagging spirits throughout my venture into the new territory of incorporating dreams into the processing of collective problems. Judith Harris generously sponsored the English translation, for which I am most grateful. For his commitment to the project and the sensitive translation, my thanks go to David Roscoe.

Thanks also to the MAS MATBAACILIK printing works in Istanbul, especially Mehmet Bora Akgül and Merve Çakıroğlu for the enjoyable collaboration.

Zurich, Spring 2014 Theodor Abt

Introduction

In this book, suprapersonal dreams, i.e. dreams that transcend the personal, are presented that relate to social issues; in other words, they are documents from the inner world which were important not only for the dreamer personally, but might also be of general interest. To enable the reader to understand why the dream world in this context is considered significant, permit me to offer a brief glimpse into my academic career.

It all started in 1972 in the Lötschental, a small valley in the canton of Valais in Switzerland, which at the time was faced with the growing threat of mass exodus into the towns and cities. As a budding engineer in agronomy at the Federal Institute of Technology (ETH) in Zurich, I was able to do my diploma thesis there in 1972. My professor, who was aware of my interest in culture and psychology, chose a topic for me based on the following question, one which was quite unusual at the time for a prospective agricultural and regional economist: "What are the chances of survival of the cultural heritage of the Lötschental?"

So I took up residence in the Lötschental and came to know the exceptionally rich cultural heritage of that area. But the topic of my diploma thesis drove me to the brink of despair, because I saw how the modern world, television, tourism, mobility were increasingly making their presence felt and might ultimately displace the traditional values and very identity of the valley.

As a typical child of my time, I started off by assuming that the chances of survival of the cultural heritage in the Lötschental depended above all on the *securing of material prosperity* and that, for example, pouring money into the local coffers would provide all that was needed to preserve this cultural heritage. So at the time, I thought that setting up specific projects leading to an improvement in material prosperity would be a suitable countermeasure to the threatened loss of identity. Accordingly, on the basis of an initial survey, I went on to analyse the socio-economic conditions in the valley. In addition to training as an agricultural and regional economist, I was also training as an analytical psychologist, and so I looked at my dreams on a regular basis. In so doing, I realised that some of my own very impressive dreams were related directly to the topic I had been given. That taught me a valuable lesson. According to the dreams, the problem was apparently not a material one, but largely a spiritual and psychological one. At the heart of the whole splendid cultural heritage of the Lötschental was its religious life. If the *experience* of this underlying religious life could be renewed in some form for the people in the Valley, the continuity of their culture would be assured.

After graduating as an Engineer in Agronomy at the ETH, I was able to work as project manager on the macro-economic development concept for the canton of Uri. The commission came from the Cantonal Government of Uri at the former *Institut d'économie rurale* of the ETH. Once again I started having dreams directly related to the problem of this development concept. Working on these dream images helped me once more to broaden my much too narrow view of the world. But I also experienced for myself how difficult it is to give the inner world its full due if one is under pressure in the external world. In the hustle and bustle of modern life, it seemed to me almost impossible not to lose sight of the reality of the soul.

After completing work on the Urner development concept in 1976 and after it had been approved by the Federal Government, I wrote my thesis at the ETH about my experiences in the Lötschental and in the Canton of Uri. In addition to presenting any given external problem and a possible solution, I also – in another part of the thesis – have presented the situation in the light of a selection of my dreams which related to the specific question involved.[1] My experience has led me to believe that if dreams relate to collective issues of today's society, their meaning should be investigated, because

1 Theodor Abt: *Entwicklungsplanung ohne Seele?* Sozio-ökonomische und psychologische Aspekte der Entwicklungsplanung im Berggebiet, with a foreword by Regierungsrat Josef Brücker and a post-script by Marie-Louise von Franz. Bern and Frankfurt am Main 1978. The hypotheses presented here summarise chapters 5.2 and 5.3 of the book. The thesis was accepted in 1977 on the recommendation of Prof. Dr. Albert Hauser, Prof. Jean Vallat and Prof. Dr. C.A. Meier at the former Departments of Agricultural Sciences and of Humanities of the ETH Zurich.

they compensate the one-sided viewpoint of whoever is responsible for any given project, meaning that they balance it out. In this way, they could make a contribution to the processing of such collective issues. For me, this hypothesis was a logical consequence of the discovery of the collective unconscious by C. G. Jung, former Professor at the ETH Zurich.

In 1979, I was able to take over the teaching of Rural Sociology at the ETH and complete my post-doctoral thesis *Progress without Loss of Soul.*[2] From 1990 to 2012, I regularly gave lectures on "Archetypal dreams about environmental issues". My teaching activities led to various articles in scientific publications dealing with the possibilities of presenting collective dreams in order to deal more meaningfully with problems of our time.[3] I made the experience that dreams contain *symbolic knowledge* which can also be conveyed within the scientific context of a Technical University.

* * *

Dreams are an expression of a spirit, one which is not identical with the intellect. In symbolic form, previously unknown viewpoints enter into the field of consciousness and are thus able to point the way to a new orientation. If we look closely at the dream collection presented in this book, we are surprised at the intelligence that the dreams have to offer. Who composes these dream stories that turn out to be so meaningful on closer inspection? It is an objective "other", one that is independent of consciousness. That is why C. G. Jung also referred to the collective unconscious as the objective psyche, because this "other" functions as an objectively observable, independent counterpart. The spirit that is experienced in dreams is like a superior second personality, which, as experience has shown, has a centring effect on the individual and paves the way for an optimal development of the personality.

First and foremost, dreams provide us with a growing insight into ourselves, in that we ourselves are the protagonists in the dream. They bring

2 Bern 1983 and 1988.

3 For example: Th. Abt, "Planning without Shadow". Published in the volume of the IAAP Kongress in Berlin 1984, Einsiedeln 1986. p. 91-110; Th. Abt, "Auf der Suche nach einem Dialog mit der Natur", in *GAIA 1/6* (1992), and Th. Abt, "Psyche und Materie". Published in: *Der Pauli-Jung- Dialog,* Berlin 1995.

up important things that the dreamer is no longer – or not yet – aware of. So dreams can balance out any one-sidedness on the level of consciousness or can extend it.

But dreams can also provide objective insights. In this case, they can give us orientation with regard to external people and things in symbolic form. If they also have collective components, such dreams can be also important for society as a whole. As I was able to discover empirically on the basis of numerous so-called 'big' dreams, a valley, a region, a nation, as well as a single person, can have a distinctive sense of individuality, that is to say, can be experienced as a kind of 'personality character'.

***

The basis for writing this book was the period between 1989-1992, a time when justification for the very existence of an independent Switzerland was being questioned, especially by the younger generation: «700 years are enough!» was the provocative cry of protest from young people on the occasion of the 700th anniversary of the Confederation in 1991. It was at this time that a vote was held on the petition for a referendum on the abolition of the Swiss Army. Dreams from various people relating directly to this question of an independent, sovereign Switzerland were so striking for me as a psychotherapist that I decided to collect them. In the course of discussions with my training-analyst at the time, Dr. Marie-Louise von Franz (1915-1998), we came to the conclusion that these big or archetypal dreams had something to say not only about the dreamers personally but were also apparently able to make some important contribution to an understanding of the collective situation of contemporary Switzerland itself, of Europe and the unconscious problems generally prevailing at the time. From this collection of dreams there emerged three photocopied reports, which had been lying around unpublished.

Some 20 years later, in June 2012, I had a short dream which made it clear to me that these reports are actually as topical as they ever were. On the day before this dream, I was tidying up my archives with a colleague. Before falling asleep that night, I was debating with myself which of the projects to tackle first of those that I had lined up for when I retired as professor at the Swiss Federal Institute of Technology (ETH). The next morning I had the following dream:

No. 1, Dream about the book project:

I am holding the book with the three photocopied reports about the situation of Switzerland at that time, and am leafing through it. As I do so, I am amazed to find quite a number of my own pictures. They are carefully executed pencil drawings, all of which I had apparently done myself at the time when I was learning how to see.

In interpreting the dream, I must start off with a personal association. Many years ago, I did a Betty Edwards course based on her book *Drawing on the Right Side of your Brain*. The aim of this course was to show participants how to look properly, that is, how to 'see' in the external world and thus be able, for example, to draw a portrait of someone facing you. During the course, I did a lot of pencil drawings.

As we have learnt from dream research, dreams behave in a compensatory way to the consciousness level and like to speak of things that we have lost sight of but which would be of importance to us. Thus after the dream, it was clear to me that the top priority on my agenda should be to go back to the three reports. However, as these reports do not have any illustrations of their own, and there does not seem much point in doing any myself, the illustrations in the dream have to be understood symbolically. That being the case, the dream images seem to be pointing out to me that – thanks to those dreams – I had learnt 'to see' in a more differentiated way. That almost certainly applies to the meaning of the various related dreams I had collected, which opened my eyes to their deeper relevance.

On the basis of the dream, I once again read the reports mentioned earlier and realised – to my astonishment – that the images of the innermost soul that they contained had lost none of their significance. On the contrary, I had the impression that the archetypal dimension of these dreams extended beyond what was going on at the time and still had much to say that is of crucial importance today. That gave me some idea of why my dream is probably telling me about a book based on these reports. In my experience, dreams often provide information about unsolved questions from the previous day, and so I interpreted the dream as a demand that this book should be written, a demand, it must be said, that came as a bolt from the blue, for, left to my own devices, I would have opted for less 'explosive' material.

In the meantime, some of the dreams presented here date back twenty years or more, yet their symbolic content remains valid in that they point out something that has not yet become generally conscious. Suprapersonal dreams from times gone by can remain relevant over very long periods of time and are indicative of significant potential insight. We only need think of the visions of the great seers. But it is not just prophets; anyone can have dreams that have collective significance, as we know from many documents, tribal cultures being one example.

The dreams reproduced here have not been altered in any way; they create documents out of the enigmatic night world known as the unconscious. Looking at the various dreams compiled here conveys some idea of what is probably being activated in the background of contemporary events, and – of this I am convinced – it still merits our attention. What we can actually do with these documents in the future – and might do – remains to be seen. I will leave it to the reader to judge whether the symbolic expressions of unconscious nature, as we encounter them in this collection of dreams, have anything of current relevance to say about the questions being raised today, not just in Switzerland but also in Europe and, more generally, about the problems facing us in this day and age, or whether they may be past their 'sell-by date' and should be relegated to the archives of the past.

***

As modern civilisation no longer turns to collectively significant dreams as an aid to orientation, **Part I**, prior to my own dream collection, will contain a selection of dreams from the early days of the Third Reich. These dreams are a verifiable example of the fact that dreams from the suprapersonal or collective background of individuals can convey an idea of things that could also have been of significance for the society of those days.

Part II deals with dreams which were collected in the years 1980-1990. The text is a new version of the first of the three aforementioned reports, written in the years 1990/91. The dreams presented there were collected by myself while discussions were going on in the country about the pros and cons of an independent Switzerland.

Part III, *Independence under Threat?* and **Part IV**, *Against the Surrender of Identity*, are based on the two other reports. They both show, on the basis of further dreams, the potential risk of totalitarianism. But they also show how we might be able to understand the unconscious driving force behind these dream images in their constructive and cultural sense.

Every dream comes with an interpretation. All the previous interpretations have been improved and reformulated. They are to be regarded initially as a *hypothesis*. Seeing all the documents presented here together allows readers to judge for themselves whether or not the interpretation I have given for each one is convincing. The personal aspects of these dreams are of little consequence in this context. They were processed by the people who had the dreams and as far as possible implemented them in real life.

Finally, in the **Epilogue**, the question is discussed of the fundamental problem arising from the fact that we are living in a world where the value and significance of dreams is no longer acknowledged. In the academic circles of today, any consideration given to the unconscious is of purely marginal importance. There is still no binding connection to the world beyond or to anything other than pure, unambiguous reason. The dangerous effect of the ignoring of this other reality and, conversely, the lack of awareness of the creative and constructive powers that emerge when the images of the unconscious dream world are a factor, will be presented in the conclusion. It will be described specifically in relation to Switzerland and to Europe and then finally summarised in more general terms.

Part I

A case study: German Dreams 1933-1939

1. The dream collection of Charlotte Beradt

The year is 1933. Germany's economy is in tatters, unemployment is rife. The National Socialist German Workers' Party (NSDAP) has seized power. The constitution has been annulled and the first of a whole series of decrees and bans has been issued by the new government. Yet at the time, very few people suspected what was soon to descend upon Germany with all the overwhelming force of a landslide, even though the seizure of power was already an established fact.

Were it not for the fact that we have – from the dream world – a collection of documents from the inner world of people in that country, it would not be unreasonable to assume that the whole development up to the reign of terror of National Socialism was due entirely to external factors, to economic, political and socio-psychological factors. These factors certainly played a major role, but there is a further aspect, a fourth one: an unconscious driving force from the inner world of the German people at that time.

In taking the period before the Second World War as an example, my aim is to show that the interpretation of statements made by important dreams of individuals can be represented as a way of understanding the complexities of the collective situation prevailing at the time. The advantage of historical material is that we can look back at the past, and – from a distance – judge more objectively to what extent there might be a connection between the inner world and the outer world. This helps us to explain external events in the light of these images. In her book *Das Dritte Reich des Traumes (The Third Reich of Dreams),* there are approximately 300 dreams which the journalist Charlotte Beradt had collected at risk to life and limb.[4] She was half-Jewish and initially sympathetic to Communism. But she soon realised that this ideology, too, had itself all the signs of becoming a totalitarian

4 Charlotte Beradt, *Das Dritte Reich des Traumes*. Munich 1966.

system. And at that point she rejected it. Beradt camouflaged her collection of dreams lest they should be discovered. For example, she replaced the words for Party with Family; Uncle Hans, Gustav and Gerhard stood for Hitler, Göring and Goebbels; influenza for arrest, and so on. Beradt hid the collection in the jackets of books. Later she sent the material to various addressees abroad until 1939, when she herself had to emigrate to America.[5] She published part of the collection in America during the war and the whole collection came out in Germany once the war was over. The text was then also translated into English and published under the title of *The Third Reich of Dreams*.[6]

For most people in Germany at that time, it was totally incomprehensible how rapidly National Socialism was able to spread and grow into a mass movement, sweeping aside all opposition with the inexorability of an avalanche. What was the galvanising force behind this movement? What was it that had got such a hold on these people.

5 Beradt, p. 12.

6 Charlotte Beradt, *The Third Reich of Dreams. The Nightmares of a Nation 1933-39.* Translation from the German by Adriane Gottwald. With an essay by Bruno Bettelheim, Chicago 1968.

2. Dream samples

The dream collection of Charlotte Beradt may well be able to indicate how political developments also announce themselves in archetypal dreams. In her own words, the most revealing dream examples come from the early days of the seizure of power by the Nazi regime at the end of January 1933.[7] In very vivid images, these early dreams show us the structure and essential nature of the totalitarian regime and give some indication of the totally unsuspected extent of the diabolically sinister developments that were about to unfold. Charlotte Beradt compares the dreams to a seismograph of unintentional psychic activity and writes: «Thus dream images could help to interpret the structure of a reality that is on the point of turning into a nightmare.»[8] It comes as a real shock to read of how, in the period shortly after the seizure of power, the dreams were revealing a situation which many Germans were not yet willing to see in such vivid clarity, even though the Nazis had repealed the Constitution, carried out mass arrests and built concentration camps for civilians.

We shall now take a closer look at some of the dreams from Beradt's collection. The first one is from a man in his mid-thirties (the exact time of the dream is not given):

No. 2, Dream about Hitler as a clown:

On Sundays I have to collect for the Nazis. And I think to myself: oh, forget it; I want a bit of peace and quiet; I take a blanket and pillow, but no collecting tin, and I don't do a thing. But one hour later, Hitler turns up. He is wearing lacquered, gleaming high boots, like a lion-tamer, shining mauve satin trousers, like a circus clown. He walks over to a group of children and

7 Beradt, p. 12.

8 L.c., p. 9.

bends down with insincere, exaggerated gestures. Then, with a totally different attitude, he strides over to a group of teenagers. Then to a circle of old maids, the sort that take afternoon tea, and with them he is more teasing. I start to feel uncomfortable in my position under the blanket and am frightened in case he approaches me as the representative of those pretending to be asleep and notices that I don't have a collecting tin. Meanwhile I am thinking about what sort of heroic answer I can come up with: for example: I have to be here because I know all about the concentration camps and I am against them. Hitler carries on doing the rounds. Oddly enough, the other people are not at all frightened of him; one of them even has a cigarette in his mouth when talking to him, many of them are smiling. Can that really be so?

My allotted collecting time is over. I pick up my blanket and pillow and walk down the station steps. When I get to the bottom, I look up. Hitler is standing at the top and is rounding off his appearance by singing something from an "Opera Magica", gesticulating wildly, a performance calculated solely to appeal to the public. Everyone applauds, he bows and rushes down the steps; once again I am struck by the mauve circus trousers.

I look around but there is no sign of his famous bodyguard. He just has a chauffeur, dressed in civilian clothes [...]. Maybe he isn't so bad after all .... Perhaps all my efforts to oppose him are a waste of time. Suddenly I notice that instead of my blanket and pillow I am holding a collecting tin.[9]

This dream presents us with a magical-seductive appearance of the dream figure Hitler. The effect is such that the dreamer, who is initially passive and briefly also prepared to protest, gradually falls into line at the end and suddenly is even willing to collect for the Nazis. What exactly is the magic power that lies behind the ability of this lion-tamer or circus clown called Hitler to create illusions and influence people?

We are unable to share Charlotte Beradt's conviction that this dream must have its roots in the external world of the Third Reich alone. For the wealth of experience of modern psychology has shown that dreams can also depict the suprapersonal dimension of the inner world of the dreamer himself. For everything that we dream also ultimately belongs to us, to our "internal

9 Beradt, p. 112-114.

Fig. 1: Formation of the SS Unit "Adolf Hitler".[10]

theatre". This is why this dream gives rise to the question of what force from the inner world of the dreamer himself is at work.

No matter how much of a clown Hitler looks in his satin trousers, there is something uncanny but puzzling about the way the dreamer is affected by his magic power. It could, of course, be seen as a compensatory debasement of the external Hitler. But for the dreamer, who at first is passively critical in the dream, this would probably be of less interest than the fact that Hitler exudes a magical suggestive power that can imperceptibly carry him away. We must look into its origins. Forcing people into line and wielding control over them obviously did not just come from outside; there was something in these people themselves that was present and at work. In his book *Hitler in uns selbst* (Hitler within ourselves), the Swiss doctor and cultural

10 Picture taken from *Damals,* 44/2 (2012), p. 17.

philosopher, Max Picard, among others, tried to draw attention to this underrated internal aspect of the problem of Nazi Germany.[11] The very title alone points to the inner world.

We shall now examine more closely this uncanny and magic force, again with the help of dreams from those days. For example, a middle-aged housewife had the following dream in 1933:

No. 3, Dream about the treacherous tiled stove:

A storm-trooper is standing in front of the big, blue, old-fashioned tiled stove in the corner of our living-room, around which we always sit and chat in the evening. He opens the door of the stove, and the stove, in a rasping and penetrating voice, starts to talk: every sentence we have said against the Government, every joke that we have told. My God, I think to myself, what will happen now, all the things I've said about Goebbels. But at the same time I realise that one sentence more or less doesn't make much difference; everything we have thought or said in confidence is common knowledge anyway. At the same time it dawns on me that I have always ridiculed the possibility of built-in microphones, and deep down I still don't believe in them. Even when the storm-trooper ties a strap round my wrist – he uses our dog leash – to take me away, I think that he is joking. I even say out loud: "You can't be serious, this can't be happening." [12]

In the same collection, and in a similar style, we have the dream of another housewife. (It is not clear when she had the dream.):

No. 4, Dream about the talking bedside lamp:

My bedside lamp is talking in a rasping voice, like an officer. My first thought is to just switch off the light and retreat into the darkness. But then I say to myself: that won't help: I rush off to my girl-friend, who has a dream book, and I look up the word 'lamp'; 'lamp' simply signifies "serious illness". At first I am very relieved, but then it occurs to me that these days, as a safety

11 Max Picard, *Hitler in uns selbst.* Erlenbach-Zurich 1946.

12 Beradt, p. 45.

measure, 'illness' is used as a code word for 'imprisonment'. Once again I am at my wits' end, completely at the mercy of the rasping voice even though there is nobody there to arrest me.[13]

And, as Beradt writes, a greengrocer had exactly the same dream. (The date of the dream is not given.):

No. 5, Dream about the denouncing cushion:

I dream about a cushion that has the gift of tongues and is testifying against me, with a non-stop account of our family conversations.[14]

What these three dreams have in common is the motif that the stove, the lamp and the cushion turn inexorably against the people who live with these objects. There is danger lurking in the superficial cosiness of the warm stove, the light of the lamp and the comfortable cushion; in the way we look at the world today, they are all nothing more than dead matter. But in our three dream examples it is very different. The 'dead' matter turns out to be not just surprisingly lively but is able to behave like someone very underhanded. The objects are denouncing the very people to whom they belong! When they start to live and speak, and denounce their owners in their most intimate sphere, then all Hell is let loose, in every sense of the term. And in fact from a Christian point of view, the Devil is the "Lord of the World", and thus of all matter. Jesus said in the New Testament (John 18.36): «My kingdom is not of this world.» And thus Christianity has left this world to God's adversary, the Devil. In the course of the further development of Christian civilisation, the heavenly God image was consolidated, whereas in the 19th century, the divine in Nature (trees, springs, etc.) and in matter itself lost much of its magic, with the result that Nature and matter were no longer experienced as being divine and were thus no longer venerated. We no longer have a world soul (*anima mundi*), just a world that has lost its soul.[15] In these three dreams, it is as if matter, long regarded as dead and thus no longer

13 Beradt, p. 48.

14 Ibid, p. 48-49.

15 See Th. Abt, *Progress without Loss of Soul.* Wilmette, Illinois 1989, part III.

venerated, has regained its liveliness and is hitting back as a painful reminder to Man that it – matter – exists independently in its own right and has to be acknowledged. And in these dreams, matter is allied with the Nazis, revealing itself to be part of the danger that is threatening.

One particularly revealing dream, which serves to further illustrate the greater depths of this collective problem, comes from a young girl. (The exact time of the dream is not given.):

No. 6, Dream about the guardian angel:

I dream that I wake up in the middle of the night and see that the two little angels hung over my bed are no longer gazing upwards but are looking down and watching me closely. I am so frightened that I creep under the bed.[16]

Charlotte Beradt says that the two little angels in this dream were «one of the commonly found reproductions of the putto figures of the Sistine Madonna.» And she continues: «It never occurs to her (the girl) that the angels, obviously hung up as guardians of her sleep, are watching over her – *are watching her closely* [...].»[17]

What is immediately apparent in this dream is that the growth and development of the Nazi movement was related to some sort of reversal. The little angels, which were previously looking up to a loving God, offering protection from evil, are now looking down on the earthly world. Instead of protecting the child from evil, the angels are watching her closely. This is indicative of a reversal of the Christian God image. For with the one-sided notion of a loving God in Heaven as pure goodness (*summum bonum*), the pre-Christian Nature deities, which were both beneficial and evil, were totally suppressed into the unconscious over the centuries. The dark side of God, which in the *Old Testament* was regarded as a natural part of God (one thinks of Noah and Job, for example), was, in the *New Testament*, split off from the God image and assigned to the Devil, the Lord of the World, 'world' in this sense, meaning in contrast to the *Kingdom of God*. With the Nazi movement,

16 Beradt, p. 50.

17 Ibid, p. 50 (author's accentuation).

Fig. 2: This picture is an example of the brutal and perfidious reversal of everything that had hitherto been regarded as good and right. In early April 1933, just two months after the Nazi party (NSDAP) had seized power, the Munich lawyer, Dr. Michael Segel (1882-1979), had lodged a complaint at the police headquarters about the 'protective arrest' of a client. His trouser legs were cut off at the knee and he was led barefoot through the city with a signboard round his neck that read: "I will *never again* complain to the police."[18]

the suppressed counter-position to the loving God was able to make its way to the surface, with the result that in this dream, the good little Christian angels suddenly started to look down as if keeping check, instead of upwards to the loving God. The supreme value, the God image, has apparently been turned upside down for the little angels. It is now to be found on earth in a dictator who is worshipped, in the idealisation of the tangible and concrete State, in materialism and the notion of pure race and so on (Fig. 2).

Thus the two little angels looking closely at the child now represent the totalitarian control exercised by the Nazi régime, whose ideology raised

18 Taken from the German catalogue of the touring exhibition *Lawyers without Rights. The Fate of Jewish Lawyers in Germany after 1933* by Simone Ladwig-Winter.

to supreme value all the inferior lower values suppressed by Christianity. This supreme value was the opponent of the loving God, the Devil. For the Germanic peoples, the latter is actually the pre-Christian *Wotan* turned into the Devil by Christianity. Wotan/Odin is the principal god in the Norse mythology of Edda poetry. As Rudolf Šimek writes in *The Edda*, he acts there as a father of gods, a god of war and the dead, a god of culture who brings poetry and runes, a god of magic and ecstasy with shamanistic characteristics.[19] He is the great magician and illusion artist. This helps us with a better understanding of the magical powers of the lion-tamer or the circus clown called Hitler in the first dream. It comes from the archetype of Wotan that lies behind it. As with any archetype, Wotan has not just a dangerous-demonic side that can carry people away but also a constructive, cultural side, as mentioned above by Rudolf Šimek.

In 1935, in his article *Wotan* (Collected Works 10, § 394), Jung wrote something fundamental about this archetype: «The Romans identified Wotan with Mercury, but his character does not really correspond to any Roman or Greek god, although there are certain resemblances. [...] At all events, the Germanic god represents a wholeness on a very primitive level, a psychological condition *in which Man's will was almost identical with God's and entirely at His mercy*. But the Greeks [and Romans] had gods who helped man against other gods; indeed, All-father Zeus [or Jupiter] himself is not far from the ideal of a benevolent, enlightened despot.»[20] In this connection, Jung also pointed out a specifically Germanic problem, namely the Christianisation of these peoples by the sword at the time of Charlemagne (8./9. century). Christian culture did not advance step by step, as was the case with the peoples under Roman rule, but in one gigantic leap from polytheism to monotheism. Wotan, «as the god of wholeness on a primitive level» in Jung's words, has no other deity alongside him who could stand by Man against his (Wotan's) destructive side. This is why the Germans were at the mercy of this storm god once the Christian god image was no longer sufficiently effective. As a pre-Christian god of wholeness, he corresponded to something on the lines of the down-to-earth shadow of Christ, or, in other words, the Antichrist. It was, in fact, not uncommon for Hitler to be equated with the Antichrist.

19 R. Šimek, *Die Edda,* Munich 2007, p. 48-59.

20 C.G. Jung, *Collected Works 10,* § 394 (author's emphasis and insertion).

Fig. 3: Roll-call in the Sachsenhausen concentration camp. There is a machine-gun aimed at the prisoners. If a prisoner was missing, the others were punished by having to stand to attention.[21]

This complete turnabout from the benevolence of the one-sided Christian "good God" to the fiendish control of all things can be seen most impressively in the following dream from a woman «approaching thirty, no profession, spoiled, liberal, cultured. She had this dream as early as 1933.»[22]

No. 7, Dream about the forbidden words:

A blackboard is placed on every corner to replace the forbidden street-name signs and – in white letters against a black background – lists twenty words that people are not allowed to speak. The first one is 'Lord' – It could well be that I dreamed that in English and not in German just to be on the safe side. I have forgotten the rest of them or probably did not dream

21 Picture taken from *Damals,* 44/2 (2012), p. 15.

22 Beradt, p. 23.

them, except for the last one, which was 'Ich/Self' (this word was written in capital letters).[23]

«That,» she added quite spontaneously, «would probably have been a vision in olden times».[24]

«And in fact», writes Beradt, «Vision means seeing, and the empty space between godlessness and selflessness which all the governments of the 20th century use as their field of force is seen incredibly clearly in this radical language regulation, the first commandment of which is: Thou shalt not speak the name of the Lord, and the last one forbids the use of 'Ich' (self).»[25] The clear statement that the dream is making is that the two words 'God' (the Lord) and 'Ich (self)' (individual) are to be abolished in speaking and therefore in thinking.

A parallel to this dream from a different culture can be found in the book *We* by the Russian Yevgeny Zamiatin that is well worth reading.[25] Zamiatin, an engineer, was a prominent and staunch revolutionary up to the early days of the Russian revolution in 1918 and was imprisoned on several occasions. But when he became aware of the increasingly totalitarian characteristics of the new rulers after the October revolution, he turned away from them in disappointment and, four years *before* Stalin's dictatorship, wrote the somewhat eery Utopian *We*. In it, he describes our world 200 years later. In this next world, only sound common sense and the concrete outside world prevail, and there is just one single State, the "United State". The sole ruler, the so-called benefactor, uses his administration to ensure that there is enough of everything for everyone. In this State, however, nobody is entitled to have an opinion. Everyone is on the same wavelength: *We is good, I is of the devil*. Dreams and love not arranged by the State are referred to as illnesses, and the term *soul* belongs to the vocabulary of the not yet enlightened, backward ancestors. The supreme value is no longer God but the dictator, and the individual Self, being of the devil, must also be wiped out. There is something terrifying about the analogy between this Utopia and the dream presented here.

23 Beradt, p. 23.

24 Beradt, p. 23.

25 Yevgeny Zamiatin, *We*, New York 2012 (reprint).

The religious problem can be seen even more clearly in a later dream by the same woman:

No. 8, Dream about the opera 'The Magic Flute':

I am sitting in a box at the opera house, which is huge, row upon row. I am beautifully attired, elegantly coiffured, wearing a new dress and enjoying many admiring looks. My favourite opera – 'The Magic Flute' – is being performed. After the line "that is certainly the Devil" a row of policemen come marching in, heading straight towards me, footsteps resonating loudly. They have ascertained from a machine that with the word 'Devil' I thought of Hitler. I see myself begging for help from all the people in their finery. They gaze rigidly ahead in silence. No trace of pity in their faces. However, the old man in the next box looks kind and sensitive, but when I try to look him in the eye, he spits at me.[26]

The motif of the machine that can control thought processes is similar to the dream motifs of dreams 3-5, the stove, the lamp and the cushion. In this dream, the police simply appear as the body which carries out the instructions of the machine that has the ability to read thoughts and uncover and denounce blasphemous thoughts about the Führer. What this means psychologically is that at the point in the *The Magic Flute* "Ah that is certainly the Devil"[27], ego consciousness in this dream is isolated from all other contents of the psyche and is thus unable to function. On this occasion, it is not a stove, a lamp or a cushion that denounces the woman, but a machine. Machines are objects produced by human beings in order to help them; ultimately they are an extension of human consciousness. But here, what happens to human beings is like what happens to the sorcerer's apprentice in Goethe's poem of the same name:[28]

26 Beradt, l.c. p. 25.

27 When searching for Pamina, Papageno meets her and her guardian Monostatos. Both men are very frightened by the appearance of their counterpart and run away in panic and fear. ("Hu, surely that is the devil! Have pity! Spare me! Hu! Hu! Hu! ...."). Papageno calms down first and then flees with Pamina . It is remarkable that the dream has the henchmen come in when both see the devil in their counterpart.

28 J.W. Goethe, "Der Zauberlehrling", written in 1797.

«I cannot break free
of the spirits I called upon.»

The aids turn into tyrants; technical progress and thus the potential to control has developed to the point where not even thoughts are free. We learned about how matter showed solidarity with the Nazis – and I deliberately repeat this – in the earlier dreams about the stove, the lamp and the cushion. Between 1946-1948, almost as a continuation of what the world had experienced under the terror of the Nazis, George Orwell wrote *1984*. In this uncanny vision of the future of a State under total surveillance, he also describes the desire to resist authority as a *thought crime*.[29]

This brings us to the central aspect of Charlotte Beradt's whole dream collection, namely the attempt to destroy the independence of individual consciousness and its relationship to the unconscious. On this subject, here is a very early document from a young man in the summer of 1933:

No. 9, Dream about the ban on dreaming I:

I dream that my dreams are only about rectangles, triangles and octagons which somehow all look like Christmas pastries, because dreaming is forbidden, of course.[30]

Given Beradt's difficulty in collecting dreams because many people were afraid to talk to her about a dream, it is all the more amazing that she heard the following dream in a similar form half a dozen times (!):

No. 10, Dream about the ban on dreaming II

It is forbidden to dream and yet I still do so.[31]

In addition to the dreams listed above, we have a large number of very similar dreams in Beradt's collection, all pointing to the fact that what

29 G. Orwell; *Nineteen Eighty-Four*, London 1949.
30 Beradt, p. 53.
31 Beradt, p. 10.

had until now been a repressed autonomous complex, known as the Devil or – to the ancient Germanic peoples – as Wotan, has now itself swept aside the autonomy of the ego complex and, accordingly, individual consciousness.

The depression of the early 1930s led to a strong desire for a new order. At the same time, the sense of having been insulted by the Versailles Peace Treaty added fuel to the feeling of a need for reparation, a need to "be somebody again". What is more, the democracy of the Weimar Republic no longer seemed able to deal with the huge problems of unemployment. So when someone came along in this desperate situation and boldly stated: "I will take on the responsibility and bring salvation", earning tremendous applause from the crowds, it paved the way for a take-over of power and *Gleichschaltung* – forcing people into line – and was tantamount to national slavery, as is shown in the dreams collected by Beradt.

Essentially this meant that the unconscious driving force that was being activated in Germany at that time could be seen in the dreams of the people living there. It is the overpowering force of the matter that was rejected by Christianity and thus became devilish which now tyrannised people and was impossible to check. This force of the inferior, the depraved – and thus the anti-Christian – was able to assert itself like a collective, autonomous complex, thanks to its suggestive powers. In this unconscious driving force, which triggered off a huge wave of passionate-diabolical enthusiasm, we recognised the Wotan archetype. As dreams compensatorily point to something that people are not aware of, we can conclude from the dreams presented here that this archetype must obviously be taken note of.

But as with any archetype, Wotan does not only make people obsessed and blind but can also have, paradoxically, an edifying and structuring effect by creating constructive images of a new, inner, holistic order. As we know from the experiences of the history of mankind, and as has been demonstrated for years in contemporary depth psychology research, so-called 'big' dreams are of significance not only for the dreamer but also for the larger collective. Such dreams illustrate what is having an effect in people's collective unconscious psychological background, as we have been able to see in Beradt's dream collection.

Unfortunately Charlotte Beradt collected the dreams of those in her immediate environment only after Hitler had seized power. This meant that any possible insights that might be gained had no influence on what was going on at the time. Thus the main value of the dream collection is that it acts as a *warning* for future generations. It shows with utmost clarity that the image world of the unconscious can be an indication of what is being activated in the psychological background. If it is possible to nurture these archetypal images and 'incubate' them, then in future it might also be possible to recognise such dangerous tendencies in good time, so that the following phrase does not become reality: "Those who sleep in democracy wake up under dictatorship."

In what follows, working on the basis of a new dream collection compiled over 50 years later, we shall examine what is constellated in the general human background of contemporary man. For today as well, dreams show that a strong wind is blowing – and not just over Europe – and is sweeping aside established structures and boundaries. Is this evidence that a clinging to the tried and trusted, to the tradition-bound is now a form of regressive isolation, or is it a necessary and healthy forward-looking form of self-limitation? Or is there a need to develop completely new forms and structures to restore the sense and identity of a community? To this end, we shall look at the image material from the unconscious. For it will be of decisive importance for the positive future development of their society whether or not people succeed in escaping the clutches of the possessive, demonic energy of an activated archetype and instead support what it has to offer culturally. What this requires will now be examined on the basis of a number of archetypal dreams.

Part II

Archetypal Dreams from Switzerland 1980-1990

3. Europe and Switzerland in the period around 1990

In November 1989, a vote was held on the Initiative to abolish the Army. In what was for Switzerland a relatively high turn-out of almost 70%, 35.6% of the votes cast were in favour of the abolition (1'052'442 for, 1'904'476 against).[32] For many, the result came as a surprise. A good third of those voting were in favour of the Army being abolished. When the Initiative was launched five years earlier, a large majority of the Swiss had merely smiled indulgently. Not even those with expert knowledge of the political situation believed that it represented a serious threat to our military potential.

A short while earlier, on August 19, 1989 the Berlin Wall fell after peaceful protests from the people. This led to the break-up of the Eastern bloc and brought an end to the long-standing Cold War between East and West. One of the effects of the new euphoric sense of peace was that for many people it was suddenly no longer as clear as it had been who was the friend and who was the foe. And now what was initially a tiny stream of supporters of the abolition of the Army soon turned into a raging torrent. What was particularly striking was not just the sudden swell in the rising tide of those enthusiastically in favour of abolishing the Army, especially among young people, but also the *strength of their feelings* on the subject. They were utterly convinced that with the initiative they were taking a step in the right direction and thus fighting for peace and for good. Those who were in the vanguard, the Group for a Switzerland without an Army (GSoA), called themselves the 'Bewegte' (those who were moved), because they felt that some force had galvanised them into movement. But what was it actually that had moved them so deeply?

32 Official ballot result.

The mood of euphoria and peace that prevailed in Switzerland after the fall of the Berlin Wall cannot be attributed solely to the end of the Cold War. For a start, there was also the dynamic energy of the 68 Movement, with the critical attacks of the sons of the active service generation on the bourgeois aims and objectives of their fathers, such as maximum profit-making, limitless individual mobility and an endless supply of energy. And there was a need for an idealistic counterbalance to this by way of a peace without end. Furthermore, *unconscious driving forces* also played a role, as we were able to see in Charlotte Beradt's dream collection.

In what follows, as in the previous section, we shall look at dreams – this time mainly from Swiss people. As already emphasised, it is up to the reader to decide for himself or herself whether the driving forces revealed in the dreams presented here are still exerting an influence and whether they still have something significant to say today, or whether they simply reflect and comment on the day's events at the time.

4. How the dream collection started: The dream about the water samples

Here is the first dream. It is that of a 35-year-old woman, the mother of two small children. The woman was completely taken aback by the fact that in her neighbourhood, in the run-up to the vote on the abolition of the Army, there had been a complete swing of mood in favour of it. She was perturbed to find that in conversations with her neighbours, she had the impression that she "could no longer get through to them". She missed the usual exchange of views when it came to voting.

When the voting was over, this experience of the lack of tolerance of differing viewpoints was by no means settled as far as she was concerned. On the contrary, she was still worried by what she had encountered before the voting and what she saw as the collapse of democratic argument, based on the accepted tolerance of a variety of opinions. She wondered what she could do about a situation that she regarded as alarming. After what for her was a courageous exchange of views with her neighbours on the subject, and still seeking an answer to her question, she had the following dream, two months after the voting, on January 24, 1990:

No. 11, Dream about the water samples:

I am sitting in the living-room of a farmhouse in X. There is an unusual group of people round the table. Men and women from all over Switzerland have gathered together to find out more about subterranean water. The owner of the farm, the farmer himself, has placed cider and apple pomace on the table; there is bread and goat's cheese on wooden plates.

I have brought along water samples from home, and a man well-known to me has brought spring water from his home. We are all looking for the large lake on which Europe floats. This water has healing powers and is free from environmental pollution. The group around the table partly look as though they are involved in a conspiracy, and partly like a group of initiates.

Each one tries to push forward towards this lake. Later we exchange crystal rings, each of which is decorated with a serpent's head and a bird's head.

The time of this dream, two months after the vote on the abolition of the Army, shows clearly that the dream does not relate directly to the voting but to something more fundamental. According to the dream, there are some things in our country that are not as they should be. It thus seems to be necessary for men and women from all over Switzerland to come together to find out more about the healing water from the depths, since, according to the dream, the surface water is polluted, no matter where it comes from. This is a special problem and an important one, and the solution must be sought collectively. And yet the focus is clearly on the quiet and steady research of each individual within the group. This is in sharp contrast to the fuss and commotion made by the media today, with hastily conducted opinion polls whenever a problem crops up. The distinctive feature of this group of individual men and women is their rustic conviviality, good solid fare, home-produced 'spirits' (dry cider and pomace) for the spirit, as well as mutual trust, as seen at the end in the exchanging of the crystal rings.

The object of the research is the lake on which Europe floats, and the water in the lake, which has healing powers. From a geological point of view, the pore areas of the depths are filled with water and thus form a sort of continuous water table. But of course Europe does not actually float on this ground water. That is why we have to look at what this dream is saying *symbolically*.

Let us start off with the amplification of the water in the subterranean lake. From an article by the ETH Chemistry professor, Ulrich Müller Herold, entitled "Liquidum incognitum: [unknown] flowing water", we learn that for the chemist, water is still *the* unknown liquid.[33] Müller-Herold writes: «In recent decades, at least one article a day is published on the subject of water and yet so far no conclusive molecular picture has been arrived at. The fact that this most everyday of all materials has preserved its secret, despite endless efforts in the field of research, has, in terms of psychological research, the characteristic of a form of narcissistic

33 U. Müller-Herold, "Liquidum incoginitum: [unbekanntes] flüssiges Wasser", published in *Schweizer Monatshefte,* No. 11, 2007, p. 35-36.

insult.»[34] Viewed in this light, the lake in the depths on which Europe floats can be understood as a symbol or best possible expression of the enigmatic reality of the unconscious soul with its life-giving reality, which almost defies human comprehension.

The whole evolution of Earth's inhabitants is based on water. In various cultures – in Ancient Greece or Ancient China, for example, – subterranean water is regarded as the abode of the dead, and in Ancient Egypt it is seen as a regenerating force. And healing thermal waters also spring up from great depths. Seen thus, the subterranean lake is a symbol of the collective unconscious. The 'outflow' or expression of this lake – or actually of the collective unconscious – are the archetypal streams of images from the depths of the soul, as revealed in dreams, visions and active imaginations. What is important according to the dream is that the water really must come from the depths, for it is the only water that is not polluted, the only one that has healing powers. This means that it is only so-called archetypal or supra-personal dreams that can exert a healing effect on our current situation. The healing powers of the deep water are the constructive symbols which, if understood correctly, can give us a sense of direction, thanks to which the meaning and purpose of a problematic situation can be understood. This means that we can regard the lake on which Europe floats as Europe's basic psychological foundation. Every large community needs such a foundation, which expresses itself in mythological images and is correspondingly identity-forming. The common myth on which Western civilisation has rested for many centuries is the Christian myth. Christian symbolism was able to give adequate expression to the common base in the depths of the European soul.

However, after the Renaissance, the symbol-creating activity in the depths of the soul was increasingly dismissed as completely irrelevant, so that the link with this subterranean lake and its healing symbolism was lost to us. The further development of the Christian myth, which might have kept it alive, thanks to *renewed and invigorating symbolic experiences*, was not given sufficient attention. And so, symptomatically, the First World War saw the first great wave of people leaving the Church, and after the Second World War, the increasingly empty churches laid bare more and more clearly the

34 Ibid., p. 35.

signs of fatigue in Christianity. The point and aim of this round table meeting is to make a contribution to re-establishing a link to the subterranean water. This is all about a connection to the lake in its present state, taking note of the changed situation in the collective background on which Europe floats. Hence the water samples.

The task facing every individual round the table is his personal search for access to this subterranean lake. And apparently there already exist samples of the water. It says in the dream that the meeting is partly a sort of conspiracy and partly a sort of initiation. The word conspiracy is a noun related to the verb to conspire. This implies secrecy and the determination of the group to do their utmost for a common cause. For Swiss people, this may also evoke memories of the myth of the founding of the Confederation. However, this is not just a conspiracy but also an initiation into a secret. There is an atmosphere of consecration about the whole thing: for every one of them it is all about the search for the healing water; it is togetherness in the service of a higher entity. This indicates clearly that their motives are not those of self-interest. When one looks at it this way, the group around the table is not just serving the Confederation. Applied to Europe in general, the dream seems to be saying that it is their duty to take care of this healing water on which Europe floats. What that means is psychologically examining the symbolic knowledge from the unconscious, the new dominant symbols of a common European culture. This involves addressing a *psychological sharing of responsibility* for Europe as a whole, a Europe in which Switzerland is firmly embedded.

The dream concludes with the exchanging of crystal rings, decorated with a serpent's head and a bird's head. We are familiar with the custom of exchanging rings for engagements or marriages. As the ring has no beginning and no end, it has been a symbol of a balanced and all-connecting wholeness since time immemorial, and is thus one of the oldest images of God. And so this exchange is the expression of a reciprocal obligation in the name of wholeness.

In the dream, the ring is made of crystal, meaning that it is made up of a body, the atoms or molecules of which are not arranged at random but in a crystal lattice. In former times, people used to believe that crystals were frozen water in the bowels of the earth (the Greek word *krystallos* means ice). In some countries in Western Europe, certainly in Switzerland, clear crystal was a means of protection or fortune telling. Crystal is the "precious stone of the Swiss mountains". The symbol of the crystal ring seems to point to the eternal within the ephemeral aspect of human relations and to the steadfastness of this group of Swiss citizens.

The rings are decorated with a bird's head and a serpent's head. Birds are able to fly. For human beings, there has always been something miraculous about this and so it became a symbol of something spiritual. The dove, for example, is a symbol of the Holy Spirit for Christians, and with the Ancient Romans, the observation of birds in flight was a way of foretelling the future. By way of contrast, the creeping serpent is a decidedly earthbound creature. Its venom can be fatal, and yet, paradoxically, the serpent can also provide the remedy, as seen in the emblem of the staff of Aesculapius. Even today, it still serves as a symbol for chemists, doctors and pharmacists. The ring, decorated with the head, the more intellectual aspect of these two animal symbols, thus points to a union of the opposites of a volatile "higher spirit" with that of the earth or matter, the "lower spirit". These opposites are also to be found in each individual. Viewed thus, each individual at this table brings to the meeting the symbol of his crystallised union of opposites, his own established personality.

This human connection creates absolute mutual trust, which is obviously essential for this research into the healing water. Here, too, we have a union of opposites. Earlier there was talk of «a personal search for access to this subterranean lake», but here the focus is on exchanging experiences. This reinforces the recognition of their suprapersonal character. Somehow the exchanging of these personal rings – symbols of a union of opposites – creates a very close connection between those present, so that it seems to be obvious to all that the individual different water samples will be of help to each of them.

What is remarkable is the fact that the potential field of tension between the people as individuals at the round table and as part of the collective group presents no problem at all. It is obviously not about who has brought the right or the best sample, and it is clear that the various water samples complement and thus complete each other.

In the section that follows, individual "water samples" will be presented, some from Switzerland but also some from other countries.

5. The seriousness of the situation

As stated earlier, back in 1990, many people felt that they were living in very peaceful times. They found it hard – if not impossible – to imagine that Switzerland could possibly be attacked by enemy forces. Yet in the suprapersonal, archetypal dreams of psychologically healthy people, it was striking how often there was talk of a generally very dangerous situation. The following examples, selected from many, will illustrate this.

The dream is that of a young woman, a well-known politician at federal level, who was mainly concerned with security policy. The day before the dream she had been involved in discussions about the Army. This is a woman who seldom remembered dreams, yet it immediately struck her as such an important one that she had written it down at once. It was the summer of 1990.

No. 12, Dream about 'futuristic' military vehicles and a chalet:

I am in a chalet in the country, with a group of total strangers. The place reminds me strongly of the village where I live. The chalet is situated on the side of the village where the anti-tank obstacle is located. The atmosphere is peaceful.

After a while, I leave the house with a man who somehow holds a key position within the group. This man is also a stranger. When we come to a fork where the lane to the chalet leads into the through road, I look down and see a column of 'futuristic' military vehicles coming towards us and I realise at once that this is a serious threat. Then, looking up, I notice that from the other side of the through road, a similar column of military vehicles is moving towards us, so that we are trapped in the middle. The man I am with is either captured or killed by the military. I myself flee back to the chalet in the hope of finding protection from the attackers. Just as I arrive, the chalet is totally destroyed by a salvo of gunfire from the military. All of us, the whole group, are killed. I wake up drenched in sweat.

The initially very peaceful atmosphere in the (typically Swiss) chalet means that nobody even remotely suspects that danger is imminent. This is then indicated by 'futuristic' military vehicles. In other words, the aggressor has assumed a form never seen before, and the threat comes from two directions, from above and below. We can say that symbolically the threat from above, comes from a higher, spiritual sphere, and the one from below, from a lower, earthly-material sphere. The danger from above, from the mental sphere, points to the threat of an ideological, fundamental blindness such as we witnessed, for example, in connection with Nazi Germany. By way of contrast, the danger from below points to an unexpected and hitherto unknown concrete danger that is heading inexorably towards us. It is not clear from the dream what exactly this threat might be. All that is shown is the merciless destruction.

Fleeing into the protection of the (typically Swiss) chalet would be *a retreat into traditional structures*, but apparently it serves no purpose whatsoever. Only an early recognition of the danger would be useful in providing protection and resistance in this threatening situation. The dream seems to be clearly compensating an all too optimistic assessment of the situation by the dreamer, an expert in security policy. This dream played a role in a strategic leadership exercise which was carried out in the autumn of 1992 (SFU 92). It was put on as a general defence exercise involving civilian and military leaders. The slogan inspired by this dream – *Thinking the Unthinkable* – played a key role in all this. But it would be foolish to narrow down this dream with the 'futuristic' military vehicles just to traditional-style unexpected military attacks. "The unexpected often happens" is a phrase that must be borne in mind here in every respect. Just think of a campaign of well-planned terrorist surprise attacks which, especially in a very cold winter, could bring our highly vulnerable consumer society to a standstill, hugely dependent as it is on power supplies.

The 30-year-old woman, who had become very involved in the campaign for the abolition of the Army, by way of making a contribution to the culture of non-violence, was also very surprised when she had the following dream on April 21, 1990.

No.13, Dream about the street of eternal peace:

A fanatical persecution and eradication of certain people (Green/Red) is being carried out by the 'Blacks'. I am one of those being pursued. As we were in the minority, we attempted to make a stand by using our wits. I tried to make my escape up a path in the woods like others before me. The path had a name, something like "Street of Eternal Peace or Eternal Hope".

At some point, we were all taken prisoner. They led us into a room and we all had to stand in rows. The figures were all dressed in the same type of black coat and black cap, and each of them had a pistol in his hand. There was one man allocated to each person in the row. They lined up in front of us and, apart from myself and two others, shot us down in cold blood, which I could hardly believe. I went to one of the figures lying on the floor, who must have been my friend. I touched him and could not believe that he was dead. We survivors were led away. I was grief-stricken and horrified.

The dreamer described herself as an idealist with green-red loyalties, and she associated the Street of Eternal Peace with the Tian'anmen Square of Heavenly Peace in Peking. There, in June, 1989, a non-violent demonstration for freedom and peace was brutally mown down by tanks, and unarmed students, even young children, were gunned down.

Like many other opponents of the Army, the woman, with her sense of goodwill and her active commitment to the cause of goodness, was also totally convinced that evil and aggression could be completely eradicated. So in the run-up to the vote on the abolition of the Army, those in favour insisted that aggression was a myth in that it was a *'lie'*, meaning that if there were no social repression there would be no aggressive people. However, compensatory to the attitude of this all too pacifist-minded woman, the dream shows a picture that is very different from that of eternal peace and eternal hope. In fact, the exact opposite is the case. In the dream, the one-sided fanatical commitment to pure goodness, with the objective of achieving eternal peace among mankind, has brought destructive counterforces into play. And this devilish force proceeds to assert itself with terrible brutality. This brings to mind the beginning of the First World War, when the International Workers Union unanimously decided to go on strike if there were another war, on the grounds that war is only started and waged by bourgeois military circles. On May 1, 1912 the following words were heard from the Inter-national Labour Movement: «It is a well-known fact that the proletariat acknowledges no national borders. It recognises just two 'nations' in the civilised world: the exploiters and the exploited. Capitalists always say: "We must arm ourselves because we are threatened by war!" But the International Labour Movement responds with a united cry: "Down with war!"».[35] Yet two years later, the First World War broke out and thousands of workers became soldiers, some of them voluntarily. «No more war» was also the slogan of the pacifists in the Weimar Republic 1919-1933. In the Thirties, there was a lot of talk of the great peace. Quite a few people in Switzerland wanted to see a reduction in Army numbers. In fact, well-intentioned, idealistic movements can, as the dream shows, easily give rise to dangerously daemonic counter-movements. The idea of voluntary defencelessness, viewed from the instinctual basis that the dreams come from, is greeted with anything but applause. On the contrary: the dreamer has to face up to the reality of evil for what it is.

So then, as also now in the current debate on non-violent pacifism, the criticism often made is that such a form of pacifism is inconsistent and self-contradictory.[36] The radical pacifist is against violence. He will therefore not even resort to it to defend himself in the event of attack. But the law of Nature is *Eat or be eaten*. Defending oneself and one's family in whatever way is an instinctive reaction of all living creatures. That is also true for a person as an individual, to whom the compensatory dream applies here. For society at large, as opposed to the individual, the situation is, of course, more differentiated, for there we have delegated the power monopoly to the police, the military and the judiciary. Nevertheless, the individual still has the right to resort to force to defend himself if necessary. If this right is not granted, it means that in certain situations, acts of terrorism for example, it is tantamount to denying someone the right to live.

35 See also the Peace manifesto of the Basle International Socialist Congress of 25.11.1912.

36 See, for example, Jan Narveson: "Is Pacifism Self-Refuting?" in: Barbara Bleisch, Jean-Daniel Strub (Eds.): *Pazifismus. Ideengeschichte, Theorie und Praxis*. Bern 2006. p. 127.

As it says in the dream, the defenceless ones *use their wits to make a stand [...] and try to make [their] escape up a path in the woods like others before (them). The path had a name, something like "Street of Eternal Peace or Eternal Hope".*

What this means is that they resort to an idealistic philosophy in an attempt to avoid a direct confrontation with the problem of evil. At the end, they are all ruthlessly taken away or slaughtered. The notion that the reality of evil can be avoided by mere cunning and that safety lies on the "road of eternal peace or eternal hope*"* is shown in the dream to be a terrible delusion. The dreamer has to openly accept the reality of evil as such and also within herself.

In this connection, the question naturally arises of what could have been so threatening at that time without being identified. The following 1989 dream from a famous American pianist shows that there is something very threatening lurking beneath the surface in the age in which we are living, and it is still present. The American had the dream in the USA on December 7, 1989 the day before President Gorbachev arrived in New York to sign the INF treaty on intermediate-range nuclear missiles. Even then, in that situation, the feeling was still widespread that our freedom and culture were hardly likely to be endangered again. This was the dream:

No 14, Dream about the amusement park with thermostat:

I am in a sort of amusement park which is roofed over by an enormous plastic or glass bell. It is packed with dense crowds of people moving about in a very mechanical way, in a zombie-like state, their faces devoid of expression. They seem to be systematically killing each other. To my amazement, I notice that hanging on the wall of this huge structure is a sort of round thermostat. But instead of numbers, it has 30 to 40 labels which are arranged in a circle. Each of these labels describes certain social situations such as "War and Destruction" or "Religion and Ecstasy". I was not able to read most of the other labels. I had the impression that this thermostat was controlling the actions of the people under the glass bell. In other words, when the thermostat moved from one social situation to another, it affected the way the people behaved. The thermostat seemed to have been turned to "War and Destruction". I tried desperately to change the setting to one that would make the situation better so that they would stop killing each other. At first I tried "Religion and Ecstasy" but soon realised that this would lead to just as much chaos and therefore be no solution. Finally I came to the conclusion that the best label would be one with a medium setting so that nothing too dangerous could happen. I find a suitable label and the situation calms down.

Then I leave the building and come to the sea. There I see an animal that is either a fish or an otter and has its nest at the water's edge. It lashes out with its sword-like tail to prevent anyone from encroaching on its nest.

Now I go back under the glass bell, only to find that once again the people are killing each other. I see that someone must have turned the thermostat back to "War and Destruction". I wonder who it could have been, for in their zombie-like state, none of the people under the glass bell realised the significance of this thermostat. To my horror, I see that the people are killing each other with guns, albeit with guns that only shoot out a stream of air, but the victims still fall down dead. I grab the guns from the people trying to kill me and I kill them.

This dream, too, gives the impression that it is not only to be understood on a personal level but also provides insight into where the danger comes from today. According to the dream, it seems to come from the collective amusement park, from the modern "plastic bell existence" in which many people live today, sheltered from cosmic connections and contexts, an artificial consumer world that seems to be secure and comfortable. There may be perfect order in such an existence but there is no spiritual life and hence no longer any individual meaning to life.

In this dream we can see – as in a highly polished mirror – how people are being manipulated in our modern consumer-oriented society. This is how we are seen by "the other side"; this is how we are seen by the incorruptible spirit that sends us dreams. According to the dream, the danger does not just come from outside, from foreign nuclear missiles or from the destruction of the environment, but also from within, from "allowing ourselves to be manipulated" by catch-phrases or slogans. Instead of working out for ourselves what is to be done, we unconsciously let ourselves be guided by such insidiously persuasive words without realising where this magnetic force comes from that leads people to behave as part of a collective rather than as individuals. And yet, for example, people are still puzzled as to why wars are suddenly started.

The central steering mechanism of the powerful plastic or glass bell is a thermostat with words written on it, words which trigger off a reaction among the people in the room. There are just two words, catch-phrases in fact, such as are to be found in the popular press, for example. It has actually been seen for decades how the masses can be influenced by catch-phrases, especially when they are backed up by arguments making clever use of statistics. With subtle advertising techniques, interest groups of every hue can declare their view of things to be public opinion. It is easy to create the impression of representativity. It is common knowledge that hastily conducted so-called opinion polls can be hugely influenced by the way the questions are phrased, and sometimes have a suggestive effect on the results.

Given the still vastly underestimated danger of suggestibility, it is well worth trying to get to the bottom of this phenomenon. C.G. Jung writes: «The effect of the suggestion is based on the release of *an unconscious dynamis.* The more unconscious it is, the more powerful is its effect. As consciousness becomes more and more split off from the unconscious [i.e. from its psychological background], there is an increased risk of psychic infection and hence of mass psychosis. With the loss of symbolic ideas, the bridges to the unconscious are demolished. There is no longer any instinct to offer protection against unhealthy ideas or empty slogans. Reason without tradition and an instinctual basis is unprotected against any absurdity.»[37]

This is why the renewal of the living connection with the unconscious night world, with its healing symbols from the archetypal depths, is so important. The dreamer manages to turn the thermostat to a medium setting.

The dream continues:

Then I leave the eerie building and come to the sea. There I see an animal that is either a fish or an otter and has its nest at the water's edge. It lashes out with its sword-like tail to prevent anyone from encroaching on its nest.

37 See C.G. Jung, *Aion, Collected Works 9.II,* footnote to § 390, p. 247-248.

There at the edge of the sea he finds a fish or an otter. This animal has simple, instinctive behaviour patterns which we can regard as a model. He lashes out with his sword-like tail to prevent anyone from encroaching on his nest. It seems to be crucial that despite our loss of individuality in the anonymous mass, we should not lose sight of our animal base, with its instinct for self-preservation and preservation of the species. This animal can act as a reminder of how each individual group or class must be aware of the need to defend its own Lebensraum and philosophy of life.

The dream concludes:

Now I go back under the glass bell, only to find that once again the people are killing each other. I see that someone must have turned the thermostat back to "War and Destruction". I wonder who it could have been, for in their zombie-like state, none of the people under the glass bell realised the significance of this thermostat. To my horror, I see that the people are killing each other with guns, albeit with guns that only shoot out a stream of air, but the victims still fall down dead. I grab the guns from the people trying to kill me and I kill them.

In the last section of the dream, the dreamer goes back under the plastic bell and sees that the thermostat is once again set at "War and Destruction". The image of pure defensive skills shown to him by Nature no longer had any influence on him. This time the people start shooting each other with deadly effective guns. Americans have the expression *to talk hot air*. Falling into this category are lies, slander and character assassination. They can all be used to destroy people, not just psychologically but also damage them physically, even leading to suicide. Not without reason do we use the term character assassination. And this is how people's suggestibility and susceptibility to slogans and catch-phrases seems to work when the thermostat is turned back to "War and Destruction".

The dream diverts attention away from the euphoria about the disappearance of the threat of foreign nuclear missiles, thanks to the INF treaty, and steers it towards an unconscious general threat of our mindless consumer society, with its use of slogans to manipulate the way people think. But the dream offers no real solution; the dreamer is sealed off from life in the plastic bell and becomes just one of the crowd.

This is why we must turn once again to the central symbol in this dream, the circular thermostat, in other words, an apparently devilish and powerful conductor which is able to develop its own incredible dynamic. And the people in this plastic bell, *in their zombie-like state,* do not even notice it. The characteristics of the circular form, the fact that it is invisible to more or less all of the people present, and its autonomy, together with the uncanny, magical control exerted by this thermostat, show that it must be a *symbol of something divine or daemonic*. Expressed in psychological terms, it means that there is an archetype behind this symbol. Thus the suggestibility of the masses of people in this building is connected to the controls of an archetype. But which archetype is this? Who or what is independently parading these catch-phrases.

6. Camouflaging the threat

As already mentioned, what happened in 1990 was hardly perceived as in any way threatening to Western Europe and hence to Switzerland. There was at most a vague sense of unease, a feeling that the situation might perhaps not be as harmless as it seemed at first glance. Was there and is there still anything at all that could be regarded as threatening? Which archetype could pose a threat? Once again it is the dream images of the instinctual basis that provide a revealing answer to this question. The following dream, slightly condensed, comes from a young woman from Switzerland. The dream occurred on November 24, 1989, two days before the vote on the abolition of the Army.

No. 15, Dream about the figures in brown:

Together with a young farmer's wife whom I know very well, I spend an hour selling bread and cheese at the stall of the local Community Association. ***.*** *Alongside us is the stall of the Third World Shop, where the pastor and his wife are also selling goods. The pastor is of the opinion that we two should be doing more for the Asians and Africans instead of just selling bread and cheese. All the time he is talking, he fails to realise that with his heavy shoes he is standing on the hand of a child. I almost have to shout at him till he finally moves his feet. But then he merely scolds the child for not paying more attention.*

Various people of my acquaintance are wearing badges with the inscription: "Abolish the Army!" Figures in brown (Nazis) are hiding behind them, but apart from the farmer's wife and myself, nobody else seems to have noticed them.

There is a narrow path reading through an area of bogland. Visibility is poor because of swathes of mist. I can hardly see the path, but I have to find my way home.

The first thing one notices is the stark contrast between the dreamer and the farmer's wife on the one hand, and the pastoral couple on the other.

The former are selling local produce, and the latter have a Third World stall, but the two cannot work alongside each other amicably. The pastor, a pacifist known to the dreamer, ought to be concentrating on the spiritual welfare of the local people, but here in the dream he is in missionary mode, saying that more must be done for the Asians and Africans. In other words, dealing with problems in faraway places is more important than selling everyday products such as bread and cheese. Yet he does not notice that he is standing on the hand of a small child. When this is pointed out to him, he reacts aggressively towards the innocent child. He is not able to admit that he has made 'a false move'.

The symbol of the child, "just beneath us" represents all the potential development in the here and now, in the sense of new and creative possibilities in life. It stands for our own connection to the immediate future as well as for everything that has not yet become banal and lacking in creativity. The growing child offers us hope. And we are prepared to take up the cudgels on behalf of the defenceless child. By way of contrast, concern for Asians and Africans, however necessary and commendable, is not such a binding obligation. The parish pastor expects people to become involved in matters that are impersonal and in faraway places rather than help out in the Community Association with its involvement in local farming activities. With this attitude, as the dream shows, he ignores the little child, who represents the development potential, the defencelessness and the creative powers of the small individual, but he is unable to admit to the shadow side of his own behaviour. What the pastor is ultimately promoting is anonymity and hence loss of individuality, the indispensable prerequisite for making people manipulable and susceptible with slogans and catch-phrases.

Then the scene changes. In the dream, figures in brown – Nazis – can be seen hiding behind the peace-loving supporters of the abolition of the Army. The association with the other part of the dream makes it clear that lurking behind these self-styled peace-loving supporters of the abolition of the Army, which includes their church representatives, there may be an attitude that is both intolerant and aggressive. Voluntary defencelessness can, in fact, provoke unbridled aggression, for, as already stated, everything that lives in Nature has its protection and defence mechanisms. "Eat or be eaten" is the brutal reality of Nature; this is – and always has been – a harsh fact to be faced all over the world. But when an organism gives up its defence mechanism or its immune system, this 'power vacuum' is immediately filled by surrounding organisms. Bearing this in mind, we can interpret the dream image as meaning that a too idealistic form of pacifism is compensated by dangerous aggression, which is something that we were able to observe in the run-up to the voting, both with the opponents and with those in favour. The aggressive defenders of the Army, who, for example, actually sprayed the pacifists with liquid manure, and the vicious attacks on the supporters of those against the Army are a good example of this. The result at the time was the loss of a democratic discussion forum. It was replaced by a "Dictatorship of intolerance of other people's opinions".

But apart from the farmer's wife and the dreamer herself, nobody else seems to have picked up on what the dream shows to be a very dangerous aspect of voluntary defencelessness. The suggestive powers of the peace shawm (an oboe-type instrument) are probably stronger, precisely because the crowd is not able to see the aggression and the claims to power that can develop behind a peace movement and go unrecognised. The language of the dream is clear. According to the dream, the well-intentioned, idealistic movement for the abolition of Army is a cover-up or camouflage for dangerously intolerant elements – Nazis.

This connection to the Nazi Reich could also be understood as follows: apart from the militarism and inhuman anti-semitism, the Brown movement sounded most idealistic at the time. Positive and constructive ideals were propagated such as family cohesion, connection to the soil, to agriculture and to the past. And the "revolutionary comradeship" of the armed and uniformed Sturmabteilung (SA) sounded good to the ears of many people in the relatively 'socialist' oriented paramilitary organisation. During the Weimar Republic, this organisation played a key role as marshal stewards in the rise of the National Socialists by using force to shield their meetings from groups of political opponents or by seriously disrupting events organised by those opponents. The yearning of many people for ideals that would bring order, meaning and security was exploited by the Nazis for their master race and *Gleichschaltung* ideology as well as the elimination of all opposition. And by the time the whole thing had ended up in a diabolically intolerant dictatorship, it was too late to intervene.

There is a narrow path reading through an area of marshland. Visibility is poor because of swathes of mist. I can hardly see the path, but I have to find my way home.

The last part of the dream indicates the way home. It evidently refers to the difficult task facing the dreamer as an individual in finding her way home. A narrow path leads through the marshy ground; one false step and the traveller sinks into the bog. The only way to avoid an accident in this misty weather is to proceed carefully step by step. After everything that the woman has seen, it is really not easy for her to find her way back into her own 'spiritual home'. This probably applies to everyone who can see the problems arising from a too absolute, unrealistic and thus dangerous pacifism, and must symbolically find their way back to themselves.

The following dream shows even more clearly the dangerous, hidden aggression lurking behind the anti-Army group's love of peace. The dream, from August 1989, comes from an elderly Swiss woman. The previous day she had been involved in a discussion with a German woman, a pacifist Socialist, who had argued that all armies should be abolished, including that of Switzerland. But when the Swiss lady set out to justify the existence of the purely defensive Army, the pacifist suddenly became very aggressive. The following night, the Swiss lady had this dream:

No. 16, Dream about the attack by the SS-men:

I am together with a group of Swiss soldiers. Suddenly we are being attacked by SS-men. They are trying to destroy us. With a huge effort, we manage to climb to the top of a hill in order to be in a better defensive position. Once we are at the top, we are able to successfully defend ourselves.

The hill, from which there is an overview of the surrounding area, symbolically represents a higher, more conscious point of view. The dream shows that it is obviously necessary to attain a higher level of consciousness in order to be able to save oneself from being overwhelmed by this dangerously intolerant and paradoxically aggressive ideology of voluntary defencelessness. The attack is symbolised by the SS-men.

Only from a superior viewpoint (the hill) can there be any effective resistance to this ideological assault. This simple and clear dream image shows us what it is all about: the 'argumentation' of the previous evening seems to have been some sort of psychological warfare. The issue at stake in this internal debate is who will succeed in gaining the complete psychological overview. This is undoubtedly the person who also brings the dark area of the soul, the shadow side, into the equation. The woman had already been paying attention to her dreams for many years. This is why the 'water samples' mentioned earlier are so important. We need to be made aware of what is going on in the inner depths, what is being activated in man's unconscious – and in the depths of our own soul. For the suggestibility of the masses spreads itself over the unconscious. Where people are not conscious of their shadow side, they can be infected and taken over. The less I am aware of my own other side and what it is capable of, the more fanatically must I attack this other side – also within myself – and, as we know, this has never yet really worked in a constructive and convincing manner.

When our day world is invaded by driving or motivating forces (other or earlier cultures spoke of Gods) that are unconscious – and are hence excluded from or taken over by the collective, the effect is similar to that of overwhelming forces of nature. That is why in such cases we use terms such as a "flood of emotions", "political wildfire", an "avalanche" or a "landslide". If, even in our own psyche, we remain unconscious of these dormant counterforces, we can easily become monopolised by such suprapersonal powers. If I am too much right-wing liberal on the conscious level, the counter-position, which I may or may not even admit to, will be correspondingly left-wing socialist and vice-versa.

Only a superior viewpoint – one which permits an overview and which is able to see both the right and the left, the top and the bottom – can make it possible to successfully defend an aggressive, one-sided ideology.

When I decided to take a break while writing these lines, and have a short siesta, I had – which hardly ever happens in such a brief period – an impressive dream which fits in here perfectly:

No. 17, Dream about SS-beetles in the Swiss House:

I am in the Swiss House. I am clearing out a cupboard which contains the statutory Swiss emergency supplies. Almost by chance, I discover that June beetles, which I assumed had long disappeared – and which are called SS beetles in the dream – had been able to breed and multiply in droves under the bottom shelf. Quickly I rip out the shelf and crush them all underfoot. Not a single one of them manages to fly away.

In real life, of course, there is no such thing as a 'Swiss House' or "June beetles that are called SS-beetles" and stuff themselves full in store cupboards. But symbolically, the dream is saying that there are evidently dangerous undermining forces at work which can multiply amazingly quickly in the 'Prosperity cupboard'. For us, June beetles are harmless and we leave them alone. But here in the dream, these June beetles are called SS-beetles. They are anything but harmless; under Hitler the SS units were created to enforce the ideology of the Nazis with brutally cruel violence. So for us, SS, linked with parasitic beetles, immediately means something terribly dangerous, ultimately murder and slaughter.

The brown June beetle (*Phillopertha horticola*) belongs to the family of the Scarabaeidae and appears at the time of the summer solstice (Fig. 4). It is a relative of the ancient Egyptian scarab (*Scarabaeus sacer*), the sacred scarab, one of the most sacred symbols of the over 3000-year-old Pharaonic culture (Fig. 5). This beetle feeds on the excrement of herbivorous mammals. After mating, the female forms a ball made of dung, often far exceeding the size of her own body. She tucks this ball between her hind legs, buries it in the ground, lays her egg on the ball of dung, from which the larva hatches a few days later and then feeds on it. Once it has turned into a black beetle, it works its way towards the daylight. For the ancient Egyptians, it looked as though new life – the new, young beetle – was emerging from the inanimate ball of excrement in the depths of the earth.

This became a sort of symbol for the self-renewing power of the Sun, which, as it grows weaker and weaker, disappears into the kingdom of the Earth, like the dung ball of the scarab beetle, rising again the following morning, miraculously endowed with new strength. As the Sun symbolises day consciousness, the scarab beetle can be understood *as the symbolic bearer of the renewal of collective consciousness.*

Fig. 4: Phillopertha horticola, commonly known as the June beetle.

Fig. 5: An impregnated female of the sacred scarab beetle kneads a lump of cowdung into a round form, tucks it between her legs, walks backwards and buries the ball in the ground.

However, the large number of beetles crawling around in the dream points to the dissociating aspect of this archetype of the renewal of collective consciousness. With light coming onto the dark under-side, the very dangerous aspects of this archetype are recognised and, according to the dream, can thus be rendered harmless. As I can now see, the dream was compensating my own naive idea – much too one-sided at the time – which still felt that the situation could not be as serious as the previously processed dreams indicated. But today, what seems to me to be probably much more important is the insight that my dream was compensating my illusions about my own shadows, my attitude of thinking that I knew what was right and what was wrong and where to locate the evil "others". Just as we as people all bear a psychological collective responsibility for the destruction of our environment and must become aware of that, so it is that the phenomenon of the brutal, heartless SS-men is not simply a phenomenon of the past, and is not just to be found north of the Rhine. My own autonomously reproducing "SS-beetles" must all be recognised and then killed, i.e. must be rendered harmless by becoming conscious.

The real meaning of this dangerous and autonomous dissociation in the countless June beetles would be that the dynamic of this archetype is directed towards a symbolic renewal of the sun, leading to a new sunrise. That would be a renewal of the collective consciousness or fundamental attitude. From the mythological point of view, the large number of beetles

Fig. 6: Picture of the Egyptian scarab (from the tomb of Pharaoh Rameses V/VI).

must become one unit, *one* scarab, which can cause the new Sun to rise (Fig. 6). This shows the importance – above all for the individual – of the personal renewal of consciousness, thanks to a development of the awareness of one's own shadow. However, as an unconscious collective process, the myth of renewal could suddenly turn into a dangerous revivalist and renewal movement.

What the dream is referring to is left open. At any rate, it might not be a bad thing to shed more light on the "dark corners" of the "Swiss House" and firmly confront those elements which were able to multiply in the protective darkness. There seems to be a need for a development of consciousness about this threat in the Swiss House. Any passive attitude towards these forces would, however, only increase the danger of a possible collective obsession with renewal. What these symbols have in common with the dream images of Dream No. 15 about the stall of the Community Association and Dream No. 16 about the attack by the SS-men could be similar in nature to the emotional ideological mood prevailing at the beginning of the 1930s. That would be a further reminder of the question raised on page 52 about the question of which archetype might be behind the thermostat.

The archetypal background of this emotional mood needs to be examined more closely, and the following dream has something to say about this. The slightly condensed version of the dream comes from a Swiss man who at that point in time, March 1990, was intensively preoccupied with questions concerning security policy and Army reform. After the first dream, which was about reforming the Army, the man woke up, but soon fell asleep again, and had the following dream:

No. 18, Dream about the bearded wanderer:

I am with my family in my house, which somehow seems to be located on the southern slope of the Gotthard. A strong wind is blowing and it is raining heavily, but nevertheless I would like to go for a walk with my 12-year-old daughter. As we come down to the pond, the rain eases off. As we sit down on a tree trunk, we meet a bearded old man who reminds me of our neighbour, Mr X, a man with missionary leanings, a pacifist Christian who belongs to a sect. Here he is something akin to "the eternal wanderer".

He is very pleased to see us and seems to be ready to take a rest. Apparently he has come up from the south on foot, probably from Venice. His last stopping place was around Rodo Fiesso. There is also a hint of him being merry on wine, which now takes a positive turn.

The dreamer's house does not actually stand on the southern slope of the Gotthard, which means that the dream statement has to be understood symbolically. For the dreamer, the Gotthard is the very heart of the trustworthy federal identity. As the centre of so-called Réduit concept, the Gotthard was also for him a symbol of federal willingness to put up a fight. The connection of his own family and house with the symbol of the Gotthard mountain range points to an inner link between a life that has a meaning that has been personally experienced and is thus worth defending and Switzerland's own readiness to defend herself.

The curious thing about the dream is the figure of the *pacifist Christian with missionary leanings*, who appears here as the 'eternal wanderer'. The symbol of the restless wanderer is a manifestation of the Old German god Wotan. He is a familiar figure in various forms, for example as Ahasver or the 'eternal wandering Jew' in Wagner's *Siegfried*. He is a symbol for the one who is not in accord with the generally accepted image of God. And later in the dream it says that *a strong wind is blowing and it is raining heavily.* As we have already seen (p. 28), Wotan also shows himself in his possession-seizing form in storm and wind.

Here in the dream, the man with the beard reminds the dreamer of his neighbour, Mr X, a man with missionary leanings, a pacifist Christian who belongs to a sect. Here the restless wanderer appears as a good Christian. This shows us that Wotan might appear in a new disguise today, namely as a peace-loving Christian. The moving force behind this peace movement, acting as if it were Christian, is actually another form of Wotan. As an angry "berserker", this archetype suffered a defeat in Germany with the way the war ended, but it still seems to be effective.

It is true that for many people the debate about the Nazi period has gone on for far too long and is still going on. But there has been hardly any development of an awareness of what unconscious driving force was unleashed in the Nazi era. That is why the same archetype is now returning disguised

Fig. 7: Odin /Wotan, the wanderer. Picture by the Swedish painter George von Rosen (1843-1923).

in another form: as Christian pacifism. According to the dream, hiding behind the good Christian who would not harm a fly and the one who preaches non-violence, lurks Wotan, who could pave a way for himself to launch a new attack.

At this point in the dream, the bearded man appears. Apparently *he has come up from the south on foot, probably from Venice.* We find this aspect of the dream in various legends of the Alpine region. Venice, the seafaring town, was always the source of the new, of progress, cultural links, what lies beyond the known boundaries. Conversely, sailors, as "global people" were always travelling and thus rather rootless. Their home was the high seas. In the Alpine legends, walkers or students from Venice, with their knowledge of new things, can bring both happiness and unhappiness. Here in the dream, the restless wanderer from Venice probably symbolises rather the dangerous side of the realm of no roots and no boundaries

In this dream, there is something about the bearded man that suggests that he is happily intoxicated on wine. For the dreamer and for many people in German-speaking Switzerland, the South, Italy, is also associated with the good sweet wine that has been exported to the North over many generations. And it is actually true that after the fall of the Berlin Wall, one had the impression that the younger generation especially had become carried away and intoxicated with the notion of peace. «Let's do something great; let's do something for peace; let's abolish the Army!» was the "peaceful-aggressive" slogan that could be heard in the autumn of 1989. It triggered off a totally unexpected wave of enthusiasm but at the end of the day was rejected by two-thirds of the Swiss voters. Since then there has been war in the Balkans and various wars outside Europe. Despite this, people find it hard to imagine that conventional war will ever again be waged in Europe. This view is certainly a consequence of the realisation and the fear that a nuclear war would be so destructive that it simply cannot be allowed to happen. So the wish is still there, especially among young people, that there should finally be an end to "those stupid war games". The aim is to renounce the use of force. But is that realistic in the modern world?

Radical pacifism, as stated earlier, (p. 47), needs to be examined critically. Defending oneself and one's family when the need arises is a natural impulse of self-preservation and preservation of the species that is justified within culturally defined limits. In a letter to Albert Einstein written in 1932,

Sigmund Freud, who counted himself as a pacifist, wrote the following words: «...For our immediate purpose then, this much follows from what has been said: there is no use in trying to get rid of men's aggressive inclinations. We are told that in certain happy regions of the earth, where Nature provides in abundance everything that man requires, there are races whose life is passed in tranquillity and who know neither coercion nor aggression. I can scarcely believe it and I should be glad to hear more of these fortunate beings. The Russian Communists, too, hope to be able to cause human aggressiveness to disappear by guaranteeing the satisfaction of all material needs and by establishing equality in other respects among all the members of the community. That, in my opinion, is an illusion. They themselves are armed today with the most scrupulous care and not the least important of the methods by which they keep their supporters together is hatred of everyone beyond their frontiers. In any case, as you yourself have remarked, there is no question of getting rid entirely of human aggressive impulses; it is enough to try to divert them to such an extent that they need not find expression in war.»[38] And the distinguished chimpanzee researcher, Jane Goodall, made the shocking discovery that the chimpanzees she so loved and admired could be cruelly aggressive and, for example, tormented a handicapped chimpanzee and even went on to kill it.[39] What we call evil is apparently not just something discovered by human beings or created by an exploitive society; evil is evidently *part of nature itself* and thus part of each individual.

The excluded "other" or outsider in our Western civilisation, the Devil, is also ultimately the lower spirit of Nature, with its constructive and destructive forces. Just as the Devil is immortal, and cannot be removed from the world by means of voluntary defencelessness or non-violence, so it is that we cannot make destructive elements ineffective by behaving as though evil did not exist. That could turn out to be a *dangerous underestimation of the reality of the Wotan archetype,* manifesting itself in a new form of drivenness. But every archetype, as we have emphasised, has its constructive side if it succeeds in integrating the purpose of the activated energy on the

38 Letter from S. Freud to A. Einstein, September 1932. Published in: "Why war?" in *The Standard Edition of the Complete Psychological Works of Sigmund Freud.* Vol. 22, p. 211-212.

39 Personal message 2000. See also J. Goodall, *Reason for Hope,* New York 1999.

level of consciousness. This is why it is crucial not to become obsessed with this Wotanic energy but to understand the constructive, symbolic content of the archetype activated deep within. Wotan's constructive side reveals itself to be mythological in its role as the herald of destinies and the creative bringer of culture who, for example, revealed to the ancient Germanic peoples the sacred knowledge of the runes.

In the dream, the wanderer stops to rest just as he is greeted by the dreamer and his twelve-year-old daughter. To greet someone means to acknowledge and respect them. For the dreamer, the daughter signifies creative future, genuine feeling and love. She is just starting off in life, open to new ideas, able to show enthusiasm and is not just geared to things that are merely useful. That is why, after being greeted by the dreamer with his daughter, the unquiet wanderer is able to rest, and his intoxicated state takes a turn for the better, as it says in the dream. This would mean that apparently it is only with respect and spontaneous creativity that the negative Wotan can be "left high and dry". Let the following "water samples from the depths" reveal in which way this contact can have a constructive effect.

7. Constructive counter-proposals

We shall begin by presenting a dream that occurred five years before the vote was held on the abolition of the Swiss Army. It comes from a 35-year-old Swiss man who at the time was not concerned with problems of security policy and Army matters and was therefore quite surprised about the dream. The dream illustrates quite impressively how the instinctual basis is able, in images, to point to problems and ways of solving them that are supra-personal and meant to be taken seriously, problems the dreamer is completely unaware of on the consciousness level. This was the man's dream.

No. 19, Dream about the Army crossing a pass with cows:

The Swiss Army has to be led over a pass. Somehow the crossing is of decisive importance for our freedom and our Army; it is as though it leads to the Réduit. The route is not a familiar one but there is said to be an old route that has fallen into oblivion. An advance guard goes off and reports back that it is fine, even for the cows that the Army has taken along. It is evidently very important that the cows are able to do the crossing, which is why the advance guard had to check out the route. The pass leads over a wild and rocky landscape, and the destination is a valley with ecological balance, a natural balance in the ecosystem.

On their way, the Army passes a cliff where a Swiss military pilot has crashed into a rock face. In another place, they discover that all the cliffs lead into towers. They are said to be fortifications built by our forefathers.

It must be stated at the outset that from the point of view of the instinctual basis, the actual abolition of the Army is out of the question. It is rather a matter of transition, albeit a difficult transition. The fact is that today the Swiss Army has to adapt to new duties and to complex weapons systems, not just technically, but also mentally and psychologically. However, the word *Réduit* in the dream could also refer to an overall renewal of the federal determination to defend the causes of freedom and independence.

In the crossing of this pass, it is also very important – according to the dream – that the cows also make the journey. As the Swiss Army does not have any cows, they are to be taken symbolically. For the Swiss, the cow is a symbol of national identity. It represents the animal world of instinct, relatedness to the soil, everything that feeds us from the grass of the Alpine area. It seems to be of crucial importance that these factors are involved in the crossing or transition that lies ahead.

The route over the pass leads into a valley where there is ecological balance, as it says in the dream. This indicates firstly the general area on which the defence army can base their operations, whereas the fact that the cows have to go with them must be an indication rather that the balance found here is also needed in the Army itself. The constant presence of the cows could refer to the consideration and attention to be given to the nature of the inner animal. Only if these inner animals are present is one generally nourished and satisfied and able to sense a connection with something suprahuman, the "holy cow" of Switzerland.

What would it mean if such a goal were to be set for the Swiss Army? The non-stop flow of technological innovations has forced the Army to update itself. One of the main problems is the fact that in many areas, military service has thus become scientifically abstract, and most of the demands made are of a highly technical or electronic nature. But if the individual members of the Army are forced to carry out the defence of their country almost exclusively with technical appliances, they are bound to lose some of their personal motivation, and then, in symbolic terms, the "internal" cows are no longer involved. In other words, what is in danger of getting lost is the inner drive, the mental and psychological motivation as a nurturing basis for the readiness to defend one's country. The dream indicates that a permanent balance needs to be found for the Swiss Army, between the increased use of technology on the one hand, and natural basic constants of those in the Army on the other. These constants also include their psychic motivation, their powers of endurance, their willingness to serve the community.

The question still remains of the meaning of the old abandoned path which makes it possible to cross to the "modern Réduit", to the valley where there is ecological balance. It would be reasonable to assume that this path to ecological balance corresponds to the empirical science of old, paying very close attention to images and signs that come from the "other side".

Habentibus symbolum, facilis est transitus (with the aid of the symbol, the crossing is easy).[40] This is an essential point of the wisdom of the ancient Nature philosophers. The well-known symbolic rites of passage (see: *Les rites de passage* by Arnold van Gennep) show us that the understanding of symbolic folk knowledge can play a part as a tried and trusted bridge across to the other world if there is to be a successful transition to a new state. Only a link back to proven knowledge involving the constants of Nature (in this case, the mountains) can prevent a fatal collision with it. The dream motif of the military aeroplane that crashed probably points in the same direction.

According to the dream, at one point all the cliffs lead into towers, reportedly the fortifications of our forefathers. Let us examine this curious motif more closely. The soaring cliff tower, understood as a symbol, can be seen as the image of an outstanding, fully-fledged personality in comparison with other people. The cliff towers as fortifications of our forefathers would indicate that probably we essentially owe our freedom to the fact that certain individuals among our forefathers learned how to come to terms with nature, be it the steep and rugged mountain world or in their dealings with their fellow-men in the process of a democratic shaping of public opinion. As a result, they became outstanding, mature personalities, firmly anchored in the suprapersonal basis of their own indestructible psychic nature.

So according to the dream, it appears to be particularly important not to lose sight of the origins and essentials of these natural prerequisites of Swiss independence, be it the almost forgotten path into the valley of (ecological) balance or the protective fortifications of nature and the mountains. In Schiller's *Wilhelm Tell* (Act I, Scene III), speaking to the forced labourers of farmers and craftsmen who had to build a Habsburg stronghold to bring to an end the imperial freedom of the towns of Central Switzerland, Tell says:

> *What hands have built, my friends, hands can destroy.*
> *(Pointing to the mountains.)*
> *That home of freedom God hath built for us.*

40 J. D. Mylius, *Philosphia reformata*, Frankfurt a. M. 1622, p. 182.

The following dream, from a Swiss man who at the time was intensively preoccupied with the issues arising from the Initiative about the abolition of the Army, also points to the central significance of knowledge from the past. The dream occurred on February 10th, 1988:

No. 20, Dream about two and two instead of five:

I am with Mr X. He draws my attention to a place in the Rütlibrief. It says: «Our strength lies in the fact that we come together as two and two, not as five.» At the time, that was a decisive turning point with regard to the freedom and the independence of the Confederation.

The dream stresses the importance of the individual connection from person to person. This is undoubtedly where the strength of the Confederation lay, for as we know, it could never come up with large numbers of people. The few who, according to the legend, met on the Rütli meadow, all knew each other personally and the occasion was – again according to the legend about how Switzerland came into being – the drawing up of the Rütlibrief. A really lasting bond can only be formed when there are just two people involved. Just how important such a bond is when serious danger is imminent, can be seen in the following excerpt from a letter from Karl Schmid, who later became Rector of the Federal Institute of Technology (ETH) in Zurich. On June 28, 1940, after the Germans had already marched into Paris, he wrote to his wife, Elsie Attenhofer, from the Gotthard area, where he was stationed:

«What is going on abroad has really hit me hard. I have just heard on the radio about the Russian-Rumanian stories. What is happening this year is apocalyptic. There is just one thing that is not affected by the terrible way in which things are rapidly deteriorating: the connection between a few, between two […].» 50 years later, Elsie Attenhofer, to whom the letter was addressed, wrote in her memoirs: «The connection between two. What importance is attached to these lines, what they mean to me today …. I had no idea at the time.» [41]

41 Quote from E. Attenhofer, *Réserve du Patron*, Stäfa 1989, p. 158.

It is appropriate at this point to recall a central idea of the teachings of Heinrich Pestalozzi: «The facilities, measures and educational aids that are set up for the sake of the masses and the crowds and their needs as such, are – regardless of whatever shape or form they assume – simply not what education is all about. In thousands of cases, they are of no use at all and are, in fact, a stumbling block to education. *Essentially the human race only educates itself on a personal level, face to face, from heart to heart.* It basically does so in close, little circles that gradually expand in grace and love, security and trust.»[42]

Just how vital a lasting one-to-one relationship can be for little Switzerland in recent times is impressively illustrated by the following: After the failure of the Disarmament Conference of 1932 in Paris, the then Head of the Federal Military Department, Federal Councillor Rudolf Minger, with his unerring sense of foreboding, had a premonition of the danger threatening Europe. Strictly in confidence he told his friend, the Divisional Commander Henri Guisan that he had him in mind as General in the event of war. As a result, Guisan was systematically prepared for the role by the Military Department, including being sent to Rome and Paris on official visits. The idea behind this was to make Guisan's name known abroad and, conversely, to allow him to become familiar with foreign armies, which, seven years later, turned out to be extremely valuable. In 1939, at the beginning of the Second World War, Henri Guisan was elected General by Parliament. As can be ascertained today in retrospect, the trust that two people shared at a time when danger was looming was crucial to the preparation of our national defence.

In order to understand the symbolic meaning of a meeting of five, we need to examine the number five more closely. The symbolism of the number five points to the structure of the natural human being since the biological basis of the human body is characterised by the number five: five extremities, five sense organs, five fingers and five toes. As we have stated, the groups of five thus point to natural man with his inborn need to be part of a trusted small group. However much each person needs this, the dream tells us that the real strength of our State system lies in the *lasting connection between*

42 H. Pestalozzi, *Ideen,* Zurich 1927, p. 187. (Accentuation by the author).

individuals. The dream seems to be reminding us of that. The fact that the dream is about the value of the relationship between two people indicates that there is a general lack of awareness about that. Thus it is definitely to be understood as compensation for the way the modern world devalues the importance of the individual and his individual connection to another human being. And there we have two symbolic statements from the unconscious about the federal willingness to take up arms.

From the point of view of the unconscious, the problem of the dwindling readiness to fight seems to call for a better understanding of the deeper-lying unconscious problem of the age that we are living in. This can be seen in the dream a young mother had in the night after she had sent off a Reader's Letter about the vote on the abolition of the Army. In her contribution to the discussion, she related the propagation of voluntary defencelessness to the often much too protective upbringing of children. The letter was published just before the vote on this Initiative. It makes more sense to present the letter before the actual dream.

> If the Big Bad Wolf no longer gobbles up Little Red Riding Hood.
>
> The rain is pelting down. Our children are playing in their room with a couple of neighbours' kids. I am trying to write some letters. Then the children start arguing about whether or not the wolf has eaten up Little Red Riding Hood. Our three-year-old boy comes running up to me, all excited, and begs me to tell his little friend Karin the proper version of the tale of Little Red Riding Hood. Karin had claimed that in her house the wolf never ate anyone. In a somewhat thoughtful mood, I once again tell the children the story of Little Red Riding Hood. Afterwards they fire all sorts of fascinating questions at me about the wolf. I know that I risk getting involved in a discussion with Karin's mother, but I myself am also fascinated by the Big, Bad Wolf. The next morning, Karin's mother comes round, but not to start an argument with me. Over a cup of coffee, she describes to me the following apparently paradoxical

situation: in order to protect her sensitive daughter, she had told her various fairy-tales in a "diluted form". And yet, as soon as Karin was in bed, she had been scared of wolves, witches and similar frightening figures. On the very evening after our talk about the wolf, she had peacefully fallen asleep, and only over breakfast had she told them about how exciting our 'wolf conversation' had been. A short while later, I had a similar experience with the son who is in his first year at school. In a big playground, he had seen larger than life-size figures from fairy-tales and stories. Some of them were familiar to him, but those that were not, kept him awake at night. Instead of just trying to calm him down, I told him stories in the middle of the night, stories he had not heard before and which were thus particularly frightening, and in so doing, seem to have banished the frightening figures into their own story world. He drifted off to sleep shortly afterwards. It is not just with fairy-tales that we remove the evil parts; in everyday life as well, we protect children by removing many genuine or imagined 'stumbling blocks' from their path. – Why am I saying all this? In this seemingly harmless everyday behaviour, I can see the same naivety in dealing with evil in many articles where various writers plead for the abolition of the Army. They claim that this is an opportunity to rid the world of war. To me, it is as if the wolf had exchanged the sheepskin for the feathers of the dove of peace.

After sending this letter, the woman had the following dream:

No. 21, Dream about the courageous Zurich woman:

Well wrapped up, I am making my way from the Limmat up to the Lindenhof. The rain is torrential. When I walk into Fortunagasse, I am met by streams of water. I remove my shoes and walk barefoot up the slope. The wind drives the rain into my face. The house facades are dazzingly illuminated by sudden flashes of lightning, peals of thunder rent the air around me. Finally I make it to the Lindenhof. In the centre there is a tower. Loud voices can be heard from within. Through a gap in the doorway, I can see a light. The branches of the lime-trees creak ominously.

I seem to be the only person there. As I approach the fountain, the stone statue (the courageous Zurich woman) steps down and addresses me. At first I can hardly understand her as she is speaking some ancient dialect. She hands me her shield, holds me tightly by the hand and leads me to the fountain, which is empty.

The floor of the fountain opens up, revealing a spiral staircase. Behind us, the fountain gate closes silently. In the darkness, we grope our way down the steps till we come to a door. I am dazzled and do not move. A sort of church or temple opens up before us, the walls gleaming dark gold and red. The floor is covered with beautiful carpets, strewn with flowers against a green and blue background. Between them, a fountain is splashing merrily away. Young people and children are running round in a circle and are playing with a red and gold ball.

The Lindenhof hill in the heart of Zurich is actually the original city, and it is from there that the Limmat city has gradually spread out. For the dreamer, the Lindenhof is her cultural home. In the dream, a storm is raging, with gale-force winds. What is striking about the dream is the contrast between the rain-soaked Fortunagasse and the dried up fountain on the Lindenhof. It is as if the intake of rainwater is not working properly to feed the fountain. As we have already seen, water is connected with psychological nourishment from the unconscious. And it is true that in our hardened, rationalistic-materialistic world view, the water from the unconscious flows away over the surface like water off a duck's back. We no longer have time to linger over dreams and fantasies. The result is that this water from the sky, these inner images, can no longer enter into us and give us life. On the other hand, collectively we experience sporadic flooding with overflowing emotions and emotional outbursts, although they are usually superficial and soon flow away, without feeding the public fountain, the fountain that is supposed to keep providing a supply of water. As there is no longer a connection between the upper level of consciousness and the water of the unconscious depths, the fountain with the courageous woman in the heart of Zurich also dries up.

In the dream, there is a tower in the middle of the Lindenhof, a tower that does not exist in real life. As can be seen in this dream image of the statue

Fig. 8: The fountain with the courageous Zurich woman on the Lindenhof in Zurich.

that comes to life, the dream is all about defence. The tower symbolises its "above-the-ground" aspect, as we saw in the previous dream. It represents a traditional form of the ability to defend but also a preview and overview on the level of consciousness. But according to the dream, all that can be heard is a confused babble of voices. Nothing worth mentioning seems to be emerging from the discussion on the level of consciousness. What seems to be missing is the insight into the dimension of depth, which may be indicated in the third part of the dream.

In the second part of the dream, after the tower scene, the dreamer approaches the dried up fountain. We read:

I seem to be the only person there. As I approach the fountain, the stone statue (the courageous Zurich woman) steps down and addresses me. At first I can hardly understand her as she is speaking some ancient dialect. She hands me her shield, holds me tightly by the hand and leads me to the fountain, which is empty.

In the dream, the "courageous Zurich woman" unexpectedly comes alive and steps down from the high pedestal. At first, she speaks to the dreamer in some incomprehensible ancient German dialect. It looks as though it will take a moment before the link can be established between the reality of the "stone" past and that of the present. The statue was erected in grateful remembrance of the courageous Zurich women. When Zurich waged war against Winterthur in the 13th century, so many men were lost, according to reports, that Zurich was left defenceless. Duke Albrecht I von Habsburg, Overlord of Winterthur, thus decided to capture Zurich, and stationed troops outside the city walls. In this desperate situation, the women of Zurich were said to have dressed up as soldiers, armed themselves with long spears, and shown themselves to the besieging enemy. Under the impression that somehow a strong army had been able to enter the city, the Duke lifted the siege.[43] Today the figure on the Lindenhof fountain is a reminder of those

43 From Karl Dändliker, *Die Geschichte der Stadt Zürich*, Zurich 1908, Vol. I, p. 91f. On the same page, Dändliker writes about what led up to the siege. On October 16, 1291, Zurich joined forces for three years with the imperial states of Uri and Schwyz for mutual support. Also involved were Countess Elisabeth of Rapperswil and other enemies of the Habsburgs. Zurich became the centre of the anti-Habsburg alliance.

Fig. 9: The courageous Zurich woman with flag on the fountain.

heroic Zurich womenfolk. Whatever is or is not historically true about this story, it definitely has great psychological significance as a myth, in that it demonstrates the standing of women and the feminine in general in successfully warding off intruders and invaders. In a period when the dreamer was lacking a sense of direction in the question of what was actually going on with regard to the abolition of the Army, it appears that this archetype of defence spontaneously springs back to life. Evidence of the fact that readiness to defend, and powers of endurance, as well as victory in battle, have in fact always been connected to the feminine is provided by the symbolic goddesses of war and victory, examples being the Greek Pallas Athena, Nike, the Greek goddess of victory, or the Germanic Walkyries.

In the dream, the "courageous Zurich woman" comes alive and gives the dreamer a shield. But as a statue on the fountain pillar, she has a banner in her hand, so the symbol of the shield needs to be given special attention. The shield indicates demarcation and defence, preventing personal attacks: So far and no farther! So the courageous Zurich woman with the shield is an archetypal opposite to the restless Wotan, who is no respecter of frontiers. By giving her the shield, she enables the dreamer to protect herself. In connection with the sending of the Reader's Letter the previous day, the protective shield may refer to something mental or intellectual, in all likelihood her successful warding off of ideas and ideologies that make her feel insecure. She receives this protection from the archetypal image or symbol of the female-maternal instinct, which has now come alive.

In the third part of the dream, the courageous Zurich woman leads the dreamer into the depths of the fountain, as in a fairy tale.

The floor of the fountain opens up, revealing a spiral staircase. Behind us, the fountain gate closes silently. In the darkness, we grope our way down the steps till we come to a door. I am dazzled and do not move. A sort of church or temple opens up before us, the walls gleaming dark gold and red. The floor is covered with beautiful carpets, strewn with flowers against a green and blue background. Between them, a fountain is splashing merrily away. Young people and children are running round in a circle and are playing with a red and golden ball.

This last part of the dream can also only be understood if we look at it symbolically. It is an invitation to descend into the innermost depths, to find out the main reason why the fountain has run dry. Down below, it is a mixture of Paradise and a non-denominational religious place, a link between church and temple, i.e. between Christian and non-Christian religiousness. It is a peaceful world, with young people and children, with bright light, colours, thick carpets and little flowers, an ideal world longed for by so many people, a children's world, full of the joys of life and spontaneity. Down there, young people are playing with a red and golden ball, a symbol of living and moving empirical wholeness. And also down there is the source from which water might possibly come for the dried up fountain, the healing water from the depths.

There does not seem to be any conscious link between the fountain below, the water from the world below and the fountain above. The door between the two worlds is normally closed. The problematic nature of the lack of experience and corresponding lack of knowledge of this other world seems to be the central message of this dream. In the dream, the young mother is given greater insight into the fact that there is a world above and a world below.

The yearning for a heavenly world has been an eternal impulse since the origin of human consciousness. But unfortunately the restoration of such a world in the outer or upper world is not feasible, neither as a workers' paradise of Communism nor as a 1000-year kingdom of peace on earth, controlled by Germany. Nor can it come about by means of voluntary defencelessness either. In the dream, this paradise of eternal youth, where there is no old age, illness or death, is to be found in the beyond, in the unconscious depths of the soul. According to the dream, however, access to this world with the fountain and the upper world can be regained. The dreamer concluded from the dream that it was important to link this knowledge of the beyond to the upper world once again. She saw that as her duty. This involves informing people about the dream and releasing it for publication.

But the young people and children down there in this world of the beyond are, in their eternal youth, simply playing with a red ball on the thick carpet covered with little flowers. That is the fascinating thing about the pre-conscious Paradise: eternally young, just playing, no struggling to exist. And in the years around 1968, that was *the* great attraction of the Hippie movement. The young people called themselves the flower children and really believed that there could be a world without war and injustice. *They identified with this eternal youth and their Paradise*, and felt contempt for the bourgeoisie. This dream image reminds people in Zurich of the autonomous youth centre which was set up in 1970 as a Youth House below the Lindenhof, in the so-called «Lindenhof bunker». A good two months later, it had to be closed down without anything that could become permanent having been made of it.[44] The new values of the hippies (also known as flower children) such as love, play and joie de vivre unfortunately could not connect with the world of the bourgoisie. Mutual accusations are pointless here since both sides felt they were in the right. The young people wanted to remain autonomous at all costs, with such slogans as «Don't trust anyone over 30!» and «Down with the State!». But the older generation were not in a position to integrate the values of the younger generation into their world view. And this additional dimension to the depth of the problem with regard to issues arising from the abolition of the Army is evidently what the dreamer had to see to help her better understand her own questions on a conscious level.

The dream shows clearly what can happen on the psychological level when an individual puts up a fight, as the dreamer did with her Reader's Letter: the archetypal image of the courageous woman was activated in her soul. The stone figure of the 'courageous Zurich woman' comes alive and leads her down to the roots of the dried up fountain and ultimately into the depths of the unconscious, religious problematic nature of the time. There, in the depths of the soul, where the values of Christianity connect with the values of non-Christian joie de vivre and sensuality, is apparently the place where the sought-after secret of the life-imparting spirit can be found in the symbolic form of the fountain.

The motif of the shield also appears in the following dream of a senior civil servant who was constantly confronted with awkward problems concerning the defence of federal independence and the European Union. He rarely remembers his dreams, but has a very vivid recollection of this one. Before the vote on Switzerland's possible entry into the European Economic Area on December 6, 1992, he had the following dream:

44 After the so-called Globus riots (June 1968), the city of Zurich responded to the demands of the young people for an autonomous Youth Centre and on October 30,1970 set up a Youth House in the Lindenhofbunker. However, after exactly 68 days, it was closed down in January 1971, for legal reasons, and because of drug-taking, according to Sigmund Widmer, who was mayor at the time. (See M. Huber in the local newspaper, *Tages-Anzeiger*, September 9, 2011).

No. 22, Dream about the toy railway:

I am riding in the toy railway of my childhood, which is somehow big enough for me to sit in. All at once, the track comes to an end. I get out. Suddenly the train is again as small as a toy railway. I am roughly seized and taken to an old fortress, where I am assigned the task of helping to defend it as it is being attacked by strangers. I am in the second section of the defence; my father is probably at the front. To fulfil my task, I have a spear and a shield made from a bed mattress with coiled springs that has been spread out. I wonder whether the shield will be enough to protect me.

In this dream, too, it is all about defence and the dreamer immediately connected it with the defence of an independent Switzerland. At the beginning, the man in the dream is riding in "the toy railway of my childhood" when suddenly it can go no further. The track comes to an end. Riding in the train, the daily pursuit of the path of duty along familiar lines, really is "child's play" compared with what is about to happen to the dreamer. He is roughly ordered to defend an old fortress. His father is in the front line; he himself is in the second section. The old fortress is from the past and represents a traditional value. The defence is carried out with his father. This points to something that the father and son have in common, namely the *sense of history and the continuity of the values of their fatherland.*

The worldwide unique cultural heritage of a direct democracy, with its tried and trusted armed neutrality and its effective federalist state system which, among other things, respects opposing opinions at local, cantonal and federal level and protects minorities, seemed antiquated to many people in Switzerland at the time of the dream. Instead, support was given to the idea of entry into the European Union although it is clear that many of the achievements of our significantly older and time-tested state system, with its defence-oriented militia Army would be lost. Relinquishing this legacy of our forefathers would cut the country off from its historic roots. The fact that this was the dream of a senior civil servant at federal level comes as no surprise since the problems arising from the question of defending Swiss independence are constellated specifically in the Federal Parliament, the Bundeshaus. That is a decisive battlefield in the debate on these questions.

So this dream is compensating a too optimistic attitude on the part of the dreamer and shows him in no uncertain terms that he must soon step up to the front line in defence of our cultural heritage, and that it is also up to him as an individual. What is worthy of note about this dream is the 'combat equipment'. In addition to a shield, he has a spear. If the shield – made out of a bed mattress with coiled springs – is an indication of a way of absorbing attacks, then the spear is an indication of a counter-attack.

What the dream is saying is that in the face of the attacks on Swiss independence before the vote on possible entry into the European Economic Area, it is not enough to resist attacks just by going on the defensive; counter-attacks are not only possible but actually sometimes necessary. It seems to be important to target the attacker specifically and, for example, to indicate unequivocally who is the aggressor in this psychological war. Whether or not the somewhat "passive federal policy" is an adequate response to ideological attacks – from without and within – remains an open question at the end of the dream.

8. A bridge to the future

In this section, models from the unconscious will be shown which relate to our future in general terms.

The following dream (December 4, 1989) comes from the same woman who dreamt about the "courageous Zurich woman". It is thus in a way a continuation of – or an extended response to – the dream about the "courageous woman of Zurich".

No. 23, Dream about the bridge to the future:

I am in the city of X, making my way to the house of my grandparents. My grandfather opens the door. He hugs me affectionately and leads me into his study. "What do you want to know from me this time? Don't you already have enough contact with the future"? Suddenly he is no longer to be seen.

As I sit down in an armchair, I notice a letter with the following address:

To the youth of yesterday and
The old people of the day after tomorrow

Tentatively I turn the letter over in my hands. It is not sealed. The letter says:

Dear bridge people,
Be of good courage and clever and discreet.
The bridge piers and bearings are diamonds,
The bridge consists of copper and gold wires,
Which you must first build.

With love,

We ancestors of yesterday

What we have here, literally, is something constructive coming from the unconscious. This dream is once again about the suprapersonal. The letter from the ancestors has a collective address and is not sealed. It is an "open letter". Yet it is not a public one for it is only intended for bridge people, who are called upon to be not only courageous and clever but also discreet.

The dreamer receives the letter from her ancestors in the house of her grandparents. Her dead grandfather, who hugs her lovingly in the dream, had a particularly close attachment to Switzerland. At the beginning of the Second World War, he was living in America with his family, but various dreams told him that he was needed in his native country. So in 1940, he decided to return to Switzerland with his family in order to be able to play his part in the defence of his country. Thus in the dream, the grandfather embodies a sense of responsibility and mental attitude on the part of the dreamer that combines a sense of responsibility and fitness for service, thanks to which, she is granted significant new insights.

The letter from the ancestors to the bridge builders of that generation which now has to bear responsibility leaves little to be desired by way of content. There is no misunderstanding the instructions. Here it is all about building a bridge. In general terms, bridges link the Here and There, the Present and the Future; in other words, they link opposites, for we also speak of bridging gaps or differences. With the bridge in this open letter, the writer is mainly talking about the time axis, for the letter is addressed to the youth of yesterday and the old people of tomorrow. And the brief conversation between the dreamer and her grandfather is about the future. So the letter must be about the bridge that can lead to the future.

It is the task of the bridge builders to build this crossing. It is true that we are living in an age of great insecurity, threatened by global problems such as the huge increase in the world's population, the destruction of the environment, economic uncertainty and problem arising from migration and globalisation. We simply do not know how to best deal with these enormous problems and thus create the transition to a sustainable, worthwhile future. As it is difficult to conceive of a viable path into the future, many people are questioning the meaning of life. Even back then, with young people in particular, there was a terrible sense of restlessness and lack of direction.

The letter of the ancestors does not refer specifically to Switzerland. It is about a bridge to the future in general, and the letter is apparently addressed to all those who are worried about our future, regardless of party allegiances or national frontiers. It is as if the dream were a symbolic answer to the worrying question of whether we humans will manage to make the transition to a sustainable future at all, and if so, then in what way?

The construction of the bridge is described by means of unusual symbols. The bridge piers and bearings are made of diamonds, the hardest of all precious stones. The word diamond derives indirectly from the Greek word *adámas*, meaning invincible. In various cultures, because of its hardness, the diamond became the symbol for the indestructible inner core of the personality once it has become conscious, and thanks to which, a person becomes inwardly centred and established as a fully-fledged personality. This renders him immune to the insidious influence of the dictates of fashion and cheap but catchy slogans. The foundation of the bridge into the future is evidently built by such individuals, such inwardly secure personalities. Apparently there are diamonds on "this side", i.e. in the present and also on the "other side", i.e. more in the future, for which purpose the bridge is being built. The diamonds on "this side" might be the already perceptibly consolidated individual personalities and their works from the past and the present, on which the bridge can be supported in the future. The diamonds "on the other side" are probably those people who, thanks to their intensive connection to the unconscious, can make those role-models visible which correspond to the spirit of the age to come.

The bridge is made up of copper and golden wires. Copper is an excellent metal conductor. Gold, by way of contrast, is noted for its outstanding constancy. Even in the age of classical antiquity, copper represented the goddess Venus; it is thus a symbol of love and relatedness, i.e. Eros in an all-embracing sense of the term. Gold, on the other hand, was always the metal of the shining sun, so in this respect we can regard it as the symbol of the sunlight's clear ability to make distinctions, the logos, the reasoning principle. The copper wire represents a firm 'relating wire', and the gold wire represents a clear, linear context, a sort of "golden connecting thread for major future developments". The pairing of the good conductor copper wires with the durable gold wires, the outcome of connections that have become conscious – is a symbolic representation of the basis that will be able to support weight in the future. The combining of the two basic principles – the connection-creating Eros and the reasoning principle of the Logos – creates for us the bridge into the future. Psychologically it signifies a constant combining of the facts of the day world brightly lit by the sun (Logos) with the facts of the connection-creating lunar night world (Eros). This dream seems to be a general aid to orientation in helping mankind to make the urgently needed transition into the future.

A couple of months later, on April 29, 1990, the same woman had the following dream, which shed further light on the motif of the gold wires.

No. 24, Dream about Joseph's tension screw:

The doorbell rings. The postman hands me a heavy yet small package. The name of the sender is simply Joseph. Surprised and yet curious, I open the package carefully and take out two strange tools, which, somewhat at a loss, I hold in my hands. Suddenly I am reminded of a visit to a museum in a monastery in Paris, where, in a corridor, I had seen a similar, albeit much larger tool. A friendly attendant had told me that it was a tension screw for making gold wires or threads which were formerly used in monasteries for all sorts of religious implements. I wondered whether I had been given a gold thread puller. But who would have thought that I might have needed such a thing? And who was Joseph? When I wake up, the first thing I think of is Joseph in Egypt, the son of Jacob.

These two strange packaged devices contain tension screws for producing gold thread or gold wire. It was immediately clear to the dreamer that with those screws you could make the gold and copper wires needed for the construction of the bridge in the previous dream. The sender of the package indicates what might well be meant with this producing of gold wires, for the first connection the woman made to the name Joseph was «Joseph in Egypt, son of Jacob».

This Joseph is familiar to us as the skilful interpreter of Pharaoh's dreams. Even back in those days, dreams were examined to see what they had to say about the future, so that thanks to them, one could prepare oneself accordingly. Think, for example, about the dream of Pharaoh in which he saw seven fat and seven lean cows. Joseph was able to interpret these dreams symbolically and related the number seven to seven years. According to the Bible, by paying heed to this interpretation, Pharaoh was able to stave off a major famine.[45] When it comes to producing gold and copper wires for a bridge into the future, then a tried and trusted aid is called for to produce these wires. It seems to be a gift from Joseph the Egyptian, who knows the art of the symbolic understanding of dreams. To shed more light on this motif of the understanding of producing wires, we must first learn more about the symbolism of gold and copper.

As stated earlier, gold is the metal of the sun, which every day brings light and cognitive skills. The sun, as the symbol of consciousness, has its correspondence in yellow gold, which shines towards us from the depths of the earth. According to an ancient concept from the philosophy of nature, gold was woven into the earth by the sun. This is what permits us to regard gold as something shining from the depths of the earth, referred to by Paracelsus as the *lumen naturae* (the light of Nature), meaning a potential for the development of consciousness that exists in the very substance of Nature itself. Gold would thus be a symbol for the shining, luminous quality of the eternal constants or archetypes of our psychological background.

The basic material for the gold threads is a nugget of gold made up of single grains of gold which come from the earth. Psychologically this nugget of gold corresponds to the image material that can be gathered from the inner psychological sphere, meaning dreams and fantasies in their raw state. With the aid of this handy little machine, the material is stretched into a thread or a wire. With a gold thread or cable, each one is attached to the other and they remain connected. An inspired interpretation of symbols from the unconscious makes it possible to see them in a meaningful context and also links day consciousness to the archetypal background. This gives rise to a discovery that something in man can make its presence felt that can convey *meaningful images of lasting value*. Thanks to the tension screw, the gold nugget is shaped into a linear construct. That corresponds to the essence of consciousness, which is bound to linear processes. Psychologically, this instrument thus points to the technique of the assimilation of the meaning of the world of images from the unconscious to consciousness.

45 Moses 1, 41, 1-36; The same story is also found, partly word for word, as the twelfth Sura called Yusuf (=Joseph) of the Koran. In Sura 12,100, we read: And he (Joseph) spoke: «[...] Oh my Lord, [...] you have taught me the interpretation of dreams [...]»

This experience shows modern man that something within him can convey a knowledge that is illustrative, but which must first be gently raised to the light of the day world. We have already come across quite a number of such documents and seen how the processing of the "raw form" of these inner images "with the aid of a tension screw", i.e. with the aid of the tools of consciousness, really does come close to consciousness, so that the inner images can become a "gold wire" in the sense of guide or manual, so to speak.

According to the dream, the bridge to the future can now be built, in combination with the copper wires, which presumably can be made by the second tension screw. As with the gold wires, the copper wires correspond to the newly *conscious awareness of the value of man's connectedness* to his environment and to his fellow-men. In the dream, the producing of these gold and copper wires for the bridge into the future seems to be the quiet work of single individuals, without political parties or committees being involved.

As we saw in the dream about the water samples, the healing water comes from the depths of the subterranean lake. Those were the archetypal images from the depths of one's own soul. In order for these healing images to be effective for us, they must, of course, first be scooped up, meaning that one must recall them, hold on to them and question them as to their meaning. In that dream, the basic material was the subterranean water, whereas in this dream, it is raw gold that has to be turned into wires or threads. In an alchemistic text by Zosimos from the 4th century, this combination of gold and water finds most apt expression. There he says to his pupil Theosebeia: «I swear to you by God, if you do this work correctly (with the fantasy material), you will possess a river of flowing gold.»[46]

46 Zosimos, *Muṣḥaf aṣ-ṣuwar,* Corpus Alchemicum Arabicum, vol. II.2., fol. 6a. 3-4.

Part III

Independence Under Threat

9. One-sided futurology

The main problem with any security policy is uncertainty about future developments. As has been seen again and again in history, even in recent times, the unexpected can never be excluded. The smallest event can have surprisingly significant consequences. Both reasonable, understandable actions as well as unreasonable, irrational actions can become the driving force behind future incidents. False assessments leading to wrong decisions, which in turn have far-reaching consequences, can never be discounted. Any security policy must therefore bear all eventualities in mind. In order to give due regard to the increased complexity that this entails, holistic and systematic thinking is called for.

Such an approach to judging a situation will, however, never go far enough unless it takes into consideration the workings of the human instinctual basis. As with the behaviour of animals, so it is with the behaviour of human beings that every impulse has its own allocated regulating images which give these impulses their direction and meaning. Thus, according to the circumstances, certain images can suddenly trigger off or put the brakes on latent driving forces; a case in point would be the provocative image of the wealthy Jew during the depression in the early Thirties of the last century or the white flag which, as a gesture of humility, can temper aggressive drive. When such provocative images come up against a latent driving force on the collective level, it can lead to behaviour that, being unforeseen, cannot be controlled by reason.

Such behaviour, which apparently cannot be explained rationally, can be understood and more easily predicted when we know what instincts are lurking in the collective background and what they would actually mean. Since both the drive and its regulating mechanism – that is the images that give meaning to the drive – belong to the irrational sphere of the way human beings behave and think, we can use the collective term *extrarational driving forces.* Such drives have definitely played a decisive role in world history time and again, be it in the national-socialist myth of Blood and Soil, or in the myth of a socialistic paradise on earth.

But how can we give this sphere of irrational driving forces its full due? If we are to form a necessary holistic judgement of the situation, we must find a practical way of recognising non-rational forces and understanding their meaning. A purely rational method of registering and recording this would be doomed to failure. Any scientific elucidation, with its one-sided emphasis on the rational approach, largely ignores this non-rational sphere. So contemporary futurology is overwhelmingly guided just by clearly ascertainable data, i.e. by the facts of the 'day world'. The final outcome is nothing more than scenarios of predictable developments. A holistic assessment of the situation calls for consideration of the whole human psyche. In other words, even the perceptions below the threshold of consciousness may contain important information when it comes to assessing the situation.[47] For the problem with any security policy is the inclusion of the improbable, the surprisingly unexpected (see, for example, the dream about the futuristic military vehicle on p. 44). And of course the 'night side' of the psyche must also be involved in the assessment of any situation.

Before the Enlightenment, there were, in all places and at all times, rational component analyses to assess a situation, as well as specialists who were consulted for their advice on how to understand the enigmatic facts beyond the frontiers of the clearly ascertainable; the flight of birds was studied and the movement of the planets and so on. That still goes on today, but because society frowns on such things, it is done clandestinely. How many convinced rationalists have confessed in a moment of weakness that they would visit an astrologist, consult oracles, toss coins or have cards read by a fortune-teller. As we no longer have a culture of dealing with the non-rational, it takes place in secret, unreflected and as if by magic.

Commenting on the fact that futurology has become one-sided, M.-L.von Franz writes: «Oddly enough, modern society [...] has forgotten that Nature long ago discovered a form of futurology, specifically in the instinctive behaviour patterns of animals. The hamster, the squirrel and many other animals stock up food supplies for the winter. Many animals move away from an area where an earthquake is in the offing. [...] These instinctive behaviour patterns are teleologically oriented towards a future goal. This is

47 For more information see Th. Abt: "Forschung am Wendepunkt. Zur Praxis des ganzheitlichen Denkens." In: *Landwirtschaft Schweiz,* vol. 3/5 (1990), p. 259-265.

also true of human beings. In the sphere which we today call the unconscious, we also have our behaviour patterns, which C.G. Jung called archetypes, and these patterns are also oriented towards the future. If a psychotherapist takes the trouble to study thousands of dreams of his or her patients, it will reveal that in retrospect, an amazing number of them prove to be an anticipation of future events.»[48]

In an earlier age, suprapersonal or archetypal dreams, always had a futurological significance for every society. We need only think of the dreams of Pharaohs, Caesars or even the occasional Pope. However, there are always fundamental difficulties in dealing with dreams. For example, they cannot be repeated at will. Every dream is unique, and nobody can ever prove that a dream has been dreamt exactly as it was written down. It is ultimately left to the value judgement of one's fellow-men whether or not a dream also has a relevant collective aspect and thus might have suprapersonal significance. *A dream is always a document, the meaning of which must be investigated and combined with astute understanding, or else there may be a dangerous relapse into an unreflective lifestyle.* If we keep this danger in mind, then it is necessary to take this psychological product of nature seriously and question it as to its meaning.

As each dream represents a single document, great value is to be attached to various archetypal dreams on the same theme. This makes it easier for us to ascertain what is the suprapersonal part of an individual dream statement. For example, after starting at the Federal Institute of Technology, in the summer semester of 1990, in what was at the time a new series of lectures entitled "Archetypal Dreams on the Problems of the Environment", I was able to discover that the survey of various dreams on the same theme produced revealing pointers concerning what the inner nature of man himself has to say on the problems of the environment.[49]

Observing the dreams is thus of particular interest here because on the basis of the compensatory effect of the unconscious, we can assume that the

48 M.-L. von Franz, *Wissen aus der Tiefe, Über Orakel und Synchronizität*, Munich 1987, p. 7-8. English translation: *Divination and Synchronicity*, without the foreword quoted here. The author of this book can confirm this statement from his own experience.

49 An example has been published in Th. Abt, "Auf der Suche nach einem Dialog mit der Natur", *GAIA* 6 (1992), p. 318-332.

dreams from the collective unconscious are also collectively compensatory. In other words, just as with individual dreams, archetypal dreams point to crass one-sided aspects of the collective consciousness. Archetypal dreams focus on those aspects of contemporary questions which, at any one time, have collectively been given too little attention on the conscious level.

The reader may wonder why once again in the following chapters, dreams from the past are presented that relate to the psychological national defence of Switzerland. One would be justified in assuming that with the clear rejection of the Initiative to abolish the Army in 1989, the subject would be over and done with, but that is not the case. Even if the vote on the abolition of the Army in 2013 clearly had no majority, it is still above all the *independence of Switzerland* that is facing the threat of being weakened and eroded step by step.[50] Years ago, the character of these dreams already revealed evidence of a barely visible threat of this demarcation. For this reason, the subject will be dealt with right away, for it is not out of the question that we might be misjudging the situation in Switzerland.

50 See for this the work by the University of Zurich Professor Emeritus of Law, Hans Giger, *Die verlorene Ehre der Mutter Helvetia, Politische Machtentfaltung im Fokus allgemeiner Rechtsprinzipien,* Zurich 2012.

10. Barely visible threat

Major changes in society come about gradually over long periods of time in the unconscious. This is very vividly illustrated in the following three dreams relating to a barely perceptible psychological threat to Switzerland's independence. One critic told me that it was ridiculous to talk of such a threat, seeing that we are "surrounded by friends". As we shall see, these dreams are initially about the subject of whether Switzerland actually is under threat.

In 1968, a Swiss woman, who was about 50 years old at the time and had not given that much thought to security policy, had the following dream. Although she could not understand it at the time, it made a deep and lasting impression on her. This was her dream:

No. 25, Dream about poison gas:

I am in the Rhine valley and I receive a message from the Army headquarters. It says that I am responsible and must take over the defence of Switzerland. Apparently a gas war is being planned. The enemies had already crossed the border and occupied a mountain in Switzerland, and now they were discharging poison gas. I think to myself: "As a woman, I can't possibly take on such a task. And anyway, I don't understand anything about army matters." But then someone explains to me very seriously: "When there is a war on, anyone who disobeys orders is shot." So I think, well in that case, I'd better do it. Then some likeable Swiss officers appeared, and I thought: "Let's go to the Restaurant Rössli, perhaps we can work something out together."

Today, almost fifty years later, it is easier for us to understand the symbolic meaning of this dream image of an imminent gas war. Gas is a volatile substance that is carried through the air. Unlike solid earthly material, gas is closer to the spiritual celestial pole. In the early days of chemistry, gas was regarded as the spirit of material, actually as "spiritual matter".

Poison gas is thus a fitting symbol for a dangerously aggressive spiritual substance such as thoughts, ideas and ideologies which can harm or even poison us from outside. History has demonstrated to us very clearly the alarming poisonous effects of intellectual constructs and ideologies. According to the dream, the enemies are invading the Rhine valley from the north; the ideological contamination comes from the north, from Germany or from northern Europe. That would apply to ideas and ideologies around 1968 (the woman had the dream in 1968), which, coming from the north, questioned – and thus attacked – Switzerland's independence, not least the notion of voluntary defencelessness, with the idea of abolishing the Army.

Since this dream, which occurred almost 50 years ago, an insidious form of poisoning has become more and more widespread here. In the run-up to the voting campaign about the abolition of the Army, this ideological 'gas war' became particularly obvious. This is aptly illustrated in the following quotation from that time. It is taken from the psychological magazine *Intra,* founded in the autumn of 1989, just before the Army abolition vote. In a section entitled 'Psychowar', one of the magazine editors wrote: «Swiss leaders must now stand by and watch how the petition for an Initiative (to abolish the Army) is triggering off a process that will be very difficult to halt: the undermining of our nation's readiness to fight.» And then comes a remarkable explanation for this: «What is clear so far is this: the acute risk of contamination comes from *a highly poisonous mixture of three convictions* which are rapidly gaining ground across our country. Firstly, there will be no war. Secondly, even if there is, it is not worth it or is pointless to give up one's life for anyone or anything. Thirdly, Switzerland is anyway merely an illusion from the past.»[51] In order to describe «a psychological war that has long been going on»,[52] the author uses the image of highly poisonous convictions rapidly spreading across our country. In the article mentioned, psychological warfare is actually named as such.

The similar image of a developing poison war was used in the dream 20 years earlier, at a time when hardly anyone dreamt that the danger of a poison gas was imminent in the way the mixture was described above.

51 S. Looser, "Überlebt die Schweizer Armee?" in: *Intra, Zeitschrift für Psychologie in der Gesellschaft*, No.1, October 1989, p.14 (Accentuation by the author).

52 l. c., p.13.

Who at the time would have dreamt that the readiness to defend the unity and the frontiers of the oldest and only direct democracy in the world as a spiritual and cultural legacy could be crippled by a poisonous gas? For the federal readiness to stand up and fight cannot simply be dismissed as a long-outdated illusion of our forefathers, especially when it comes to the defending of our spiritual values and our frontiers. This dream shows clearly how symbolic expressions of the instinctual base can convey knowledge of future developments.

The following dream, from the morning of New Year's Day, 1985, also goes back to the time when the question of the readiness to fight was not yet really a talking point. The Swiss man who had this dream was about 40 years old, and at the time was not particularly involved in Army matters. The Initiative concerning the abolition of the Army was still in the early stages and was more or less ignored by the dreamer. So when he woke up, he was surprised at this unusual dream.

No. 26, Dream about the Rütli Report with Major X:

In memory of General Guisan's Rütli Report of 1940, a meeting of commanding officers is taking place on the Rütli meadow. The leading officer in the Army is Major X, who has the position held by General Guisan. He is a good commander of the battalion in which I do my military service. There are roughly as many officers present as I recall seeing on the Rütli Report photograph of 1940. There are a lot of newly promoted officers who had somehow not had time to sew on the new stripes that they had apparently just received and so had simply placed them on their shoulder. This showed that the ceremony was taking place on January 1, because that is the date when promotions are made. (The same date as the dream.) Although I am only a soldier, I was also invited to take part and it somehow seems to be taken for granted that I am there. Major X asks us questions and I seem to have all the answers, and so at the end we have a conversation. It does not matter that I have no rank. Major X is very interested in what I have to say. This all makes a deep impression on me.

From the point of view of defence psychology, General Guisan's Rütli Report of July 25, 1940 was an extremely significant ritual, albeit a highly risky one, because the leadership of the Army could have been wiped out overnight. France had capitulated and little Switzerland was almost completely surrounded by the Axis powers. Federal President Marcel Pilet-Golaz had made a speech on June 25, 1940 in which he pleaded that the country should adapt to the new situation in Europe. Exactly one month later, on the Rütli meadow, the commander-in-chief of the Swiss Army, General Guisan, informed the some 420 officers, from commanding officers down to the battalions, of the intention to defend Switzerland from the Réduit in the Alps.

The officers stood in a semi-circle around the flag of the Urner battalion 87. General Guisan saluted the flag and turned to his officers. He declared: «I have made a point of gathering you together on this historic site, on ground that is the symbol of our independence, in order to inform you about the situation and to talk to you soldier to soldier. We are at a turning point in our history. The very existence of Switzerland is at stake. Here, we soldiers of 1940 will take strength from the teachings and spirit of the past in order to contemplate the present and the future of our country with courage and determination and pay heed to the mysterious call that goes up from this meadow. If we look clear-eyed into the future we will overcome the difficulties that always arise and which are described as the "deceit and guile of the time" in the Federal letter of 1291.»[53] He went on to say: «The historical events which have recently taken place before our very eyes have in no way weakened our sense of duty to be on the alert. At the moment there are more troops than ever stationed on our borders and they are excellent ones. What seemed totally out of the question a few weeks ago is now within the realms of the possible: we can be attacked from all sides. The Army has to adapt to this new situation and draw up a position that enables us to defend ourselves successfully on all fronts. In this way, she will fulfil her historic duty, which has fundamentally not changed. This is the reason for the redeployments which your units were involved in.» On the way back, the General went from one group to another, greeting each individual by name and shaking him by the hand.

53 Edgar Bonjour, *Geschichte der schweizerischen Neutralität. Vier Jahrhunderte eidgenössischer Aussenpolitik,* Vol. 7, p. 183 f.

Fig. 10: Rütli Report of July 25, 1940.

Not adaptation but unquestioning resistance was the order of the day in the Rütli Report, much to the annoyance of the dictators in Berlin and Rome. The Réduit, the French term for the retreat of the Swiss Army to the 'Alpine fortress' with the security of the Gotthard railway, was the only possible form of resistance in the face of the overwhelming superiority of the German Luftwaffe and the tank units to the north and west, as well as Mussolini's troops to the south. After the fall of France, attempting to defend the central plain with the few tanks and aeroplanes at the disposal of the Swiss Army was out of the question. Today this Réduit thinking has been strongly criticised by some people, one argument being that it would have meant simply abandoning the central plain and the large towns and cities to the enemy.[54] But this is to ignore the fact that at the time, there was more to the Réduit thinking than purely military considerations. At a time when the country was under very serious threat, the General was sending out a message

54 Details in Markus Somm, *General Guisan. Widerstand nach Schweizerart,* Bern 2010, the chapter entitled: "Rester fidèle à nous-mêmes: Entscheidung auf dem Rütli", and p.153 f.

to the dictators: we shall defend ourselves, even if the situation appears hopeless. And to the Swiss people themselves, Guisan was saying with the Rütli Report: we shall not give in but will keep the flag flying in the struggle for our independence! Guisan chose the Rütli meadow in the Canton of Uri rather than Morgarten or Sempach, for example, because according to the legend about how Switzerland came into being, this was the site of the origins of the Swiss Confederation. Three cantons came together and in the name of the Almighty, swore the oath of confederation and agreed to act jointly to defend their independence. They did this even though the situation at the time – which, of course, we can never precisely reconstruct – would scarcely have made such a step possible. The superior strength of the Habsburg Empire would have discouraged any sensible strategist from risking such a step. But the confederates counted on the protection of the Almighty. That was the preamble to their decision to support each other in the cause of freedom and independence. With these spiritual and symbolic roots of Swiss independence in mind, Guisan consciously acknowledged the reality of the soul, and it may well have been the most significant action he ever performed. He was able to counter the superior strength of larger numbers with the strength of connectedness (the personal handshake!) and the strength that results when people stand side by side, (see also Dream No. 20, the Dream of two and two people instead of five, on p. 70). This was federal-style resistance, and history has shown that in 1940, contrary to all rational thinking, it was the right way to react.

According to this dream from 1985, it seems to have been necessary once again to recall the symbolism of the Rütli Report. For since then, an alarmingly discouraging mood has become more widespread in Switzerland, something along the lines of: "We are no longer independent anyway. Who does little Switzerland think it is?" And so just a couple of years after this dream, on the occasion of the 700th anniversary of the Swiss Confederation in 1991, young people were saying: "700 years are enough." And it is true that a few years later in 1992, there was a real danger of a surrendering of identity. This could be seen when it came to voting about whether or not Switzerland should join the European Economic Area. The majority of the Federal Council, the Parliament, the trade organizations and the media were very much in favour and campaigned accordingly. It was, however, rejected as a 'colonial agreement' by the people and a clear majority of the cantons and so the threat of the «surrendering of identity» was, for a while at least, averted. Nevertheless the danger still exists of the unity of Switzerland being dissolved, as can be seen in the ever-increasing and deeper integration into international agreements.

There is no denying that there are certain benefits to be derived from these ever closer interconnections on an international level, both politically and economically, but it also means a weakening of Swiss independence. It seems to be a no-win situation: we have to join in so that we can have our say, but that will only make us more and more dependent. These are the facts if the gaze is directed towards the power structures of *this world*. The inevitable effect of such a one-sided view of matters is very disheartening and the dominant feeling will be that we have become nothing more than a 'pawn' being pushed around by those bigger than ourselves. But according to the dream, alongside these power structures, there are also certain *spiritual values* that contribute to Switzerland's uniqueness and are apparently still worth fighting for.

At the time of the report, in the summer of 1940, those who still realised what was going on knew where the Devil's work was being done. Today there are no obvious dictators in Europe. However, we must not forget that with the end of the Second World War and the ensuing disappearance of the prevailing reigns of tyranny, the mental epidemic that had spread over parts of Asia and Europe did not just vanish from the face of the earth. But when the war was over, people were so preoccupied with reconstruction work and the problem of fending off a new rule of tyranny with the Soviet Union that it was not fully possible to cultivate an in-depth awareness of what had really been going on before 1945. The roots of the forces that had seized control of the minds of the Axis Powers, (including Japan) with the ensuing incomprehensible brutality, only came to light long after they had capitulated, and even then, not fully.

The reality and the significance of the psychological background may have been seen in various places and people may have been made at least partially aware of it, for example in the New Age Movement, which talked about the dawn of a new era. And the value of connectedness was recognised and eagerly sought after by some of the younger generation. One of the slogans of the hippies in America in their protest against the Vietnam war was «Make love, not war.» But despite all this, much remained on the surface, was immature or was too esoteric and without lasting effect. The never fully acknowledged diabolical-destructive, fascist spirit which had people in its grip at that time was once again, albeit in a less obvious guise, able to grab people by the unconscious, just as we saw earlier in Chapter 6, "Camouflaging the threat" on page 53. This evidently explains why, in the dream about the Rütli Report with Major X, the Army leadership sought answers to questions on the subject of psychological national defence.

The dream image of the memory of the Rütli Report of the summer of 1940 is indicative of a significantly greater danger than might be supposed when we look at the situation in Switzerland then and today with regard to Europe. For years we have seen that in the European Union, structures have been created that have been worked out by politicians and their experts, and all that the people have been able to do, at most, is to approve them. Thus we have a European construct that may partially have a common currency but no genuinely democratic political structures. In the meantime, the centralistic structures have continued to develop unimpeded and today we all know about the dubious effects that the common currency has led to. For example, on November 6, 2011 we could read: «Media and experts advise against a plebiscite on the permanent "ESM Rescue Fund"»[55] It has become clear that the ESM is an undemocratic construct that ultimately – without the people actually realising it – has set back the liberal parliamentary structures of democracies in Europe. The idea that totalitarian conditions could imperceptibly develop in Europe is a possibility and a danger not to be lightly dismissed. There are many people who are critical of the fact that no democratic check system is in place. When just a few people can have billions at their disposal without citizens having a say in the matter, then parliamentary debates on smaller sums in the individual EU countries are reduced to being political sideshows. Their sole importance lies in lulling people into believing that democracy in their country is still working. As long as the economy is healthy, all is well, but as soon as the unemployment figures start to rise, there is a desperate cry for a firm hand. "Those who sleep in democracy will wake up under dictatorship." We have heard this sentence before, and history has taught us that it should be taken seriously.

55 Gerhard Wisnewsky, *Verheimlicht, vertuscht, vergessen. Was 2011 nicht in der Zeitung stand*, Munich 2012, p. 323.

What is impressive about this dream is to see how, even back in 1985, the danger of becoming discouraged and the renewed need to reinforce the will to put up a fight by standing by one another, becomes clear on a conscious level with such a vivid image. The choice of the dreamer's battalion commander, i.e. someone he actually knows, emphasises the importance of the *personal aspect of this cohesion*. The dreamer was made to feel that he was being addressed personally about the situation and thus went on to devote more time and energy than he otherwise might have done to the questions arising from the Initiative on the abolition of the Army.

The dream compensates the typical feeling of the individual in today's world: "I'm not going to make much difference anyway." This attitude of resignation is countered in the dream by the way it points to a basic strength of the Swiss character: in this small country, *the individual does make a difference*. The dream shows us that an individual soldier, or – as in the previous dream – an individual woman, can speak up when they have something to say about a specific question.

Both dreams, the one about the gas war of 1968 and this one about the Rütli Report of 1985, show that from the viewpoint of the unconscious, Switzerland is psychologically faced with a threat that is barely visible but which is slowly and systematically threatening to undermine its psychological powers of resistance. Whereas the dream about gas war draws attention above all to the danger of poison gas, the dream about the Rütli Report encourages people to put up resistance to the 'threat of being taken over' and to stand together. It emphasises the role of the individual as well as the importance of the relationship between individuals. In each case, the dream should compensate and rectify the over-optimistic assessment not only of the two individuals who had the dreams, but also of a larger number of people who were either unable or unwilling to see any external threat.

The following dream, from August 14, 1990, sums up very clearly a basic problem of the barely visible psychological threat to Swiss independence and comes up with an initial response to the questions raised earlier. It comes from a 56-year-old high-ranking officer in the Swiss Army. On the evening before the dream, he had had a long talk with a member of the "Schoch Study

Group on Army Reform". The main question was what needed to be borne in mind to help in understanding the crisis of confidence concerning the Army.

No. 27, Dream about the sick man with the sore:

In checking that we have taken the necessary steps for the defence of our country, containers attached to the wall are opened. As I unwrap the covers, I am amazed at how carefully everything has been packed, with fastenings made of leather and aluminium. The documents inside show the civilian authorities how the supply of munitions works in the event of war.

A man unknown to me is lying in bed. When I look at him more closely, I see that on the underside of his arm there is an unclean running sore.

The dream takes up the subject matter of the previous evening's conversation about military preparations. In the dream, there is mention of munitions and then of an unknown man. Munitions as a concrete means of defence, together with the organisation thereby involved, are a fitting symbol for readiness to defend in the material sense. So according to the dream at least, nothing seems to have been lacking in that respect some twenty years ago. Everything is as it should be.

But the "unknown man" is the problem. He is sick. In the context of checking out the military preparations, the dreamer linked this image with the "Unknown Soldier", who is a symbol of the man who has to defend himself and his country. But the man is not fit to fight. He is lying in bed and has a running sore. This would mean that when it comes to checking out the preparations, the man is the weak link. He is suffering from an infection which has to be healed, otherwise he will have blood poisoning. The problem of the dwindling powers of resistance, according to the dream, is a running, unclean sore on the underside of the arm. An open sore shows that the body's own immune system evidently cannot build up enough resistance. However, it is usually possible to heal wounds by means of hygiene and the proper treatment.

Now why is the arm the carrier of the infection? If we look into the symbolism of the arm, then the following possibility emerges as an interpretation. The arms symbolise a decisive new degree of freedom. When man no longer needed arms for locomotion, he could make free use of his hands and thus both create and use tools, light fires, attack, throw and so on. In other words, it gave him greater freedom of action. We know that parallel to man learning to walk upright and making differentiated use of his hands, there was a corresponding strong development of the cerebrum, a decisive step in the development of human consciousness. Now in the dream, a body part, one which symbolises freedom of action, is the carrier of a sore. This seems to affect the whole body for the man is bedridden. The "Unknown Soldier" needs to be given healthy freedom of action again. In this respect, something is missing that needs to be attended to if he is to become healthy and whole again.

Today, many years later, many people in Switzerland genuinely have the feeling that with the European Community, Swiss freedom of action is an outdated notion. When an individual person's life becomes meaningless, he is known to be much more easily influenced by suggestion, or, in terms of the dream, more susceptible to infection. What is true for an individual, is also true for a country: if the belief in the notion of an independent Switzerland starts to fade, so does the readiness to become involved in the *res publica* of this country and defend its values. If, for example, the militia system (The Swiss militia system refers to the fact that in Switzerland, politicians and the armed forces are not professional.) is questioned in politics and in the Army, then the country's will to assert itself will also be weakened.

The open sore is a sign that the wound was not adequately cleaned in accordance with medical regulations, which is essential if sores are to be healed. The body is evidently not capable of getting rid of foreign bodies on its own. That hinders the healing process. This brings us to a fundamental problem in dealing with foreign bodies, with which the "Unknown Soldier" is confronted and ultimately overwhelmed. The unclean state of the wound could, for example, be the confrontation of the individual with the idea of the pointlessness of establishing boundaries, and the individual can come up with no satisfactory answer to this. Time and again we hear that Switzerland must open itself up more and break down its conservative backward-looking policy of demarcation. Phrases like 'isolating oneself' and 'sealing oneself off' have become catch-phrases, although they hardly apply to the true situation in a Switzerland that is open to the world. But if such phrases are bandied about frequently enough, they do cause the 'Unknown Soldier' to be dangerously infected, thus weakening the political power to defend an independent Switzerland. For what would there be left to defend or repel if we were to allow ourselves to be swallowed up by the large entity called Europe just so that we can have a say in matters?

In their anti-Semitic propaganda, the Nazis used phrases like 'contaminated wound', 'foreign body', and 'infection'. At the time, the problem of contamination was just assigned to one specific group of people. By way of contrast, the "Unknown Soldier" is himself the problem, and he must become conscious of how he can protect himself against ideological infection, whatever its source may be.

Since the time of this dream, quite a few things have changed and, there is evidence of a certain pride in independence among the people. Nevertheless, it is safe to say that the following dream documents have lost none of their topicality.

11. Possible counter-measures

If Switzerland's conception of itself is questioned and it leads to a fading of the high esteem in which a direct democracy is held by the people, a democracy that has developed gradually and in conditions that are clearly discernible, then it is a psychological problem. If the Confederation really *is* based on such esteem, and if it is deemed worth defending by the politicians, then it follows that the counter-measures to secure it must also be of a psychological nature. It is thus of no little interest to see what psychological attitude would be appropriate from the viewpoint of the instinctual basis, the dreams.

Our next dream example, dated September 9, 1990, comes from a 28-year-old mother of two small children. What is interesting is that almost one year after the Initiative to abolish the Army had been successfully turned down, the unconscious was still preoccupied with this question in her dream.

No. 28, Dream about the Repetition Course for women: (After basic training, the military service in Switzerland consists of regular Repetition Courses)

Together with Sabine X, I was called up for a Repetition Course. We had wooden weapons that were covered with knots. We were demonstrating to Sabine's many children that these very simple wooden rods were very effective. The weapon was made of wood, either completely of wood or of wood with knots of string wrapped round it like a net, and the knots in the string created little bumps, which on the other model are made of wood. So the weapon was a completely natural product, something that any woman can make, just as she has done. But the bumps have to be there. It was possible to strike an enemy with them very effectively, both in the sense of "to hurt" and also "to conquer". To make sure that it worked in an emergency, it was necessary to practise with them in peacetime. The children were very impressed.

Even in the course of the dream itself, I had the feeling that if you practised hard with this weapon in peacetime, there would never be an emergency situation, because the others would sense that you were able to defend yourself. It is evidently very important to keep practising hard with this weapon in peacetime.

The woman was neither a member of the Women's Military Service nor was she particularly interested in Army matters. Her husband was a soldier in the Army who dutifully performed his compulsory service. She herself had no sense of aimlessness nor any lack of ability to assert herself. So she was surprised to find herself having a dream about defence. As this is apparently also a dream that cannot be understood just on a personal level, we need to examine it step by step to see what it might be saying about the subject of 'defence' on a level that is beyond the personal.

In the dream, the woman is accompanied by her friend, Sabine X, who, as the dreamer tells us, is very feminine and has a strong character. Together they have been called up for a Repetition Course, although the weapons could not be more simple. This 'dream weapon' made such a deep impression on the dreamer that she went on to make such a weapon herself, namely the model with the knots of string wrapped round it like a net. She said: «Just looking at this club gives me strength. It gives me peace. It makes me feel satisfied. The club is like a psychological weapon against everyday nonsense. It is meaningful for me. Even with such things as housework, it is important what one thinks, although it is often dismissed as stupid.»

It is amazing that this weapon could give the dreamer such a feeling of peace and be so meaningful. It only really made sense to me on September 29, 1990, a good two weeks after I had heard the dream, when I was in a Japanese mountain village and came across such a club in a shop. It was a pestle, used, for example, for crushing sesame seeds. With this so-called Surikogi, all the stumps of the branches that have been cut off are left on the thick trunk. This turns the kitchen utensil into a very effective and much-feared weapon.

The Japanese have split the ability to defend themselves into various separate disciplines. The art of Ju-Do, Karate-Do, Aiki-Do, Ken-Do and so on, consists in practising this skill so well that if possible, one need not resort to using it. The air of strength and self-confidence alone are intended to deter

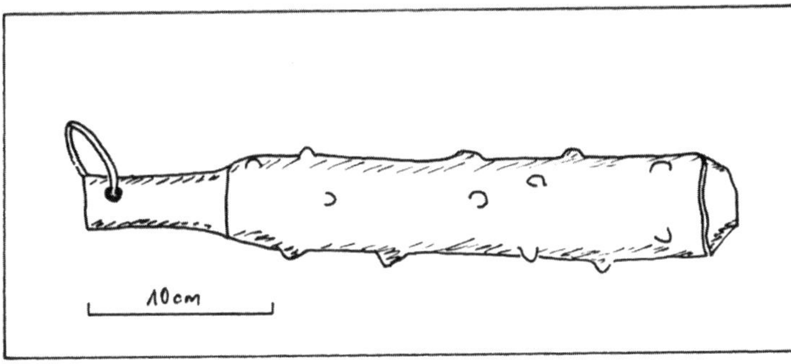

Fig. 11: A Japanese Surikogi made of Sansho-wood (author's sketch).

any potential assailant. This is probably why such a club can convey a feeling of peace and serenity. The ability to defend and the readiness to do so keep latent aggression at bay. One is more likely to be left in peace. And in an atmosphere of security, it is easier to arrive at a sense of the meaning of life when the sheer struggle to survive is not a factor. Thus this simple everyday utensil, which is so close to nature and is also an effective weapon, points to the instinct for self-preservation and the preservation of the species that is in the nature of every living creature. When I am attacked, I hit back – and with a vengeance! As a young woman and mother of small children, her basic instinct tells her that the ability to defend is simply essential, precisely because she feels the need to be able to live in peace. Did the wolf not say to the sheep: "I felt provoked!" before he tore it apart?

To get a better understanding of the 'dream weapon', we need to look at the symbolism of the staff from various angles. The herdsman today still guides his flock with a staff (crook). It points them in the right direction. Thus the staff is also a sign of leadership powers, especially in the Church (Bishop's staff [crosier]) or in the Army (Commanding officer's staff). The staff is hence related in meaning to linear, direction-pointing consciousness. The phallic form of the club points to the creative aspect, as is the case with the magic wand for example. Thus the staff embodies direction, directedness and creative ordering.

What makes the weapon special are the bumps made of knots or stumps of branches. They act as pressure spots so that any blow that is struck is many times more effective, as is the case with a spiked mace. So it is not a harmless weapon; on the contrary it can inflict pain and injury. The pieces of string with the knots would be direct connections, thought connections. This is also expressed in the fact that what has to be said is said in direct, cogent arguments, brief and to the point. When, for example, people claim today that we do not need an army because in the Second World War it was not thanks to the Army that we were spared, then the following simple words of a Landammann (local governor) from the canton of Uri are an effective response: «Of course, we (those of us who did active service) were not solely responsible for preserving our independence, but despite all other one-sided attempts to provide an explanation, we can still remain convinced today that had our Army not been prepared to fight, then in all probability there would have been at least one foreign army in our country. Even if it were only to fill a military vacuum, it would have been dangerous for all parties involved in the war. We would have lost our freedom for years to come and, as the example of occupied countries shows, we would probably have had to do active service or unpaid labour for another country, with great loss of life. For example, I recall that 12'000 young men from Luxembourg were sent to fight on the Eastern Front. The protests of the local people were quickly suppressed by means of indiscriminate shooting of hostages. A third of those who were sent never returned.»[56]

The handy club, about 50cm long, is light, can easily be carried around and any woman can make one herself. It is almost a primeval weapon, such as was used in the Stone Age. According to the dream, each woman can make the defence weapon in her own way. This is diametrically opposed to the modern notion that "The ability to defend oneself" must be delegated to a High-Tech army of well trained professionals. As this kind of defence weapon is probably less suitable for physical 'close combat', the symbolic meaning of the "Repetition Course for women" with this 'dream weapon' is probably the cultivating and exercising of a *psychological form of defence*.

Indeed, the dreamer experienced this herself when she made one of the 'dream weapons': «The club is like a psychological weapon against everyday nonsense. It gives my life meaning.» Those were her words. For

56 Speech by former Landammann Josef Brücker on the occasion of the Diamond Jubilee celebrations on September 2, 1989 in Altdorf, duplicated, page 10.

her, it was a helpful symbol, pointing her in the right direction. In accordance with the previously mentioned law of compensation, dreams generally point to areas that have been neglected on the level of consciousness. Thus the fact that in the dream the women are practising defence together on a Repetition Course is probably pointing out that more attention must be given to the value of the psychological national defence carried out by women.

Generally speaking, women embody the backbone of the will to fight. Fighting to protect wife and children is a fundamental law of nature. And if the woman behind the man is doggedly defence-minded, the man is able to fight courageously and confidently. In Schiller's *Wilhelm Tell* (1.3), the Stauffacher woman calls out to her Werner: «Look forwards and not backwards!», and thereby gives him moral support. And we have heard of various battles where the women have rushed to the aid of their men dressed in soldiers' uniforms and have turned the tide in their favour. As stated earlier, the Godhead of war is usually a woman (Nike, Victoria, Walkyrie and so on). It surely makes sense if the information on security policy and national defence is formulated in such a way that women feel that their issues are being expressed more and heeded. For young women and mothers are the very people who sense instinctively how precarious their situation and that of their children would be if peace did not reign. Time and again, in recent times as well, we have seen the terrible effects that war can have on the civilian population. The surest guarantee that such a threat does not suddenly become reality is still the existence of a credible army of one's own that can create a feeling of security and strength.

According to the dream, psychological resistance must take root in the individual households, for the term Repetition Course indicates that the use of the 'dream weapon' must be practised time and time again by large numbers of women. Voluntary defencelessness would, of course, be fine by the women and mothers if the enemy soldiers were different and, in the event of war, treated young women and children with consideration, did not steal, rape and murder. The realisation of the effectiveness of sound common sense, which sees through such wishful thinking as illusory, must evidently be worked on constantly by *women among themselves,* according to the dream, so that one can retaliate should the need arise. If this is not clear and attacks are made in debates and in the media on our readiness to pursue an independent policy of demarcation without it being possible to respond swiftly with forceful and specific counter-attacks, then such undermining attacks on the individual and collective readiness to defend are allowed to proliferate because no conclusive arguments are forthcoming, not even around the family table. According to the dream, the feeling of having an independent defence force would be very pleasing to the whole family:

It says in the dream: *Even in the course of the dream itself, I had the feeling that if you practised hard with this weapon in peacetime, there would never be an emergency situation, because the others would sense that you were able to defend yourself.* And *The children were very impressed* by this simple defence measure in an emergency… .

The following dream from an old Swiss woman also seems to be offering advice on how to deal with ideological attacks. She was very worried about the rise in religious fundamentalism all over the world. The dream occurred in October 1990.

No. 29, Dream about wild dogs:

I am standing somewhere. A pack of large dogs comes running up to me. I also have a large dog with me. He moves towards these other dogs, wagging his tail in a friendly way. But the dogs go berserk and attack him wildly. He runs away. I breathe a sigh of relief at least I'm safe now. I can leave before they return.

Then I turn into a trinity. I am myself, but am also an English soldier called Tommy as well as an American with no name. We address each other as "we", but we are identical. We are in the Saudi Arabian desert. Then the pack of mad dogs comes rushing towards us with bared fangs. They are rabid and we know that all is lost. We take out our cameras and decide to photograph the dogs as they attack us so that when our remains are found, people will be able to see what has happened to us. Then we stand there calmly and click. The dogs stop short because they think it is a new secret weapon. They turn round and run off. We pick up our guns and fire away at them. Tommy says: "Now we are safe." And tears come into his eyes because he is so relieved.

The dream is a representation of the right way to deal with mad dogs in the Arabian desert. In the pack of large dogs in that part of the world, the dreamer saw the aggressiveness of the tyrant of Baghdad, Saddam Hussein. In August 1990, his troops had marched into Kuwait. Exercising his superior military strength, Saddam Hussein had conquered the small country of Kuwait, having previously instigated a pointless war with heavy losses against the neighbouring country of Iran. As was the case with Hitler, his terrible lunacy led to hundreds of thousands of deaths. In 1990, this man was probably the most famous – or rather notorious – example of a man possessed by a devilish ideology. As of January 1991, a coalition was set up, led by the USA, legitimised by a resolution of the UN Security Council to liberate Kuwait by military means. According to the dream, the best defence mechanism against the pack of aggressive dogs is not to panic but to stay cool, calm and collected and to take photographs. In other words: to remain objective (camera lens objective!). An example of that might be the determined attitude of the coalition at the time. When Saddam Hussein offered to negotiate but without giving up Kuwait, Margaret Thatcher, the British Prime Minister simply said: «That's pathological.» In one sentence, she said what had to be said. That is what photography does: naming things as they are in clear objective language. Not emotional, but down-to-earth.

But what is the connection between this problem of how to deal with fanatical conviction and Swiss national defence? On December 15, 1990, as I was working on this report, Federal Councillor Kaspar Villiger was taking part in a programme on Swiss Radio: the Samstagsrundschau, (the Saturday Review). Commenting on his situation as Head of the Swiss Military Department (EMD), he said: «At the moment, I feel as though I am surrounded by vicious wolves.» And one could certainly gain this impression by following the voting in the National Council on December 13 on the Parliamentary Investigation Commission concerning the so-called P-26. The P-26 was a secret resistance organisation of some 400 soldiers who, in the event of Switzerland being conquered by the Warsaw Pact countries, were to organise resistance. In the Chamber of the National Council there was talk of a secret army and the one responsible for this resistance organisation was publicly insulted as being a Putsch general. The impression that was created really was that the Federal Council was "surrounded by vicious wolves". Quite a number of parliamentarians in Switzerland had definitely lost all sense of proportion.[57] But it must be borne in mind that at more or less the same time, the data filing (the compiling of registration cards) of some 700'000 was also uncovered, which, of course, added to this emotional one-sidedness.[58]

When people are apparently fanatically and aggressively one-sided in what they believe, as was the case in the debate on the Resistance organisation P-26, then we must conclude that they have fallen into the clutches of an archetype. Then we must take a photograph, as the dream image shows, meaning that we must try, as objectively as possible, to establish what the roots behind such an attitude are: what is the driving force behind such strong emotions, which can sweep aside any arguments that contradict one's own view of the matter? Let us see what conclusions we can draw from the above dream image that would help us to deal with such excessive emotions. This would mean that as far as possible, an objective and calm attitude is called for in such a case.

57 In the announcement about Martin Matter's book *The Secret Army that was no Secret*, which came out in 2012, it says: «The secret Army P-26 came to light in 1990 and was liquidated in disgrace. For the first time, this book tells the true story of the resistance organisation, whose members have done nothing to be ashamed of.» In some cantons, the members were belatedly honoured.

58 The official aim of the data filing was to protect the country from externally directed subversive activities that might destabilise the system and lead to the establishment of a totalitarian Communist dictatorship.

12. Where do we get our courage from?

To deal effectively with the questioning of Switzerland's independence, what is needed in the debate, as we established in the previous chapter, is a determined readiness to take defensive action, and, where necessary, strong and specifically targeted counter-attacks. But where are we to take our courage from? What could serve as models in the counter-offensive against these undermining forces? To be able to answer this crucial question we need to remind ourselves of the foundations of our State system. For just as the defence system of an individual collapses if his existence no longer seems meaningful to him (Dream 27, p. 104), so it is that a country's readiness to defend itself also fades if there is no general sense of a strong national identity. So the decisive question is: Is Switzerland more than a 'Super Monaco', i.e. more than just an expedient association existing solely for the purpose of maintaining the common welfare? The dreams of Swiss people, both men and women, also have something to say on this subject.

The following dream, from August 12, 1990, comes from a 36-year-old Swiss woman. Over the previous two years, she had been very worried about the country's future. When she wrote down the dream, she said it was as if everything «was still buried deep. I woke up as if from a deep, a very deep sleep.» We can therefore assume that this dream is about a 'water sample' from the depths of the collective soul.

No. 30, Dream about the Gotthard crystal:

From someone unknown to me, I receive a sort of three-dimensional puzzle made of stones and keys which together make up the outline of Switzerland and correspond in number to our cantons. Each canton is made out of a stone, which, of course, is shaped like its outline. And although the stones are all different, visually they form a whole.

As with an Asiatic puzzle, there is an end stone, and if this one stone is missing, the whole thing collapses. This key to the puzzle is a splendid, naturally formed, pyramid-like rock crystal in the shape of a key. It replaces the Gotthard Massif. Instead of the bit, this Gotthard-key-crystal has small crystals which link together from below in the cantonal stones, so that all the cantons are attached to each other and kept together. If it were not for the Gotthard-crystal-keystone, the cantonal stones would fall apart because they would not be connected to each other.

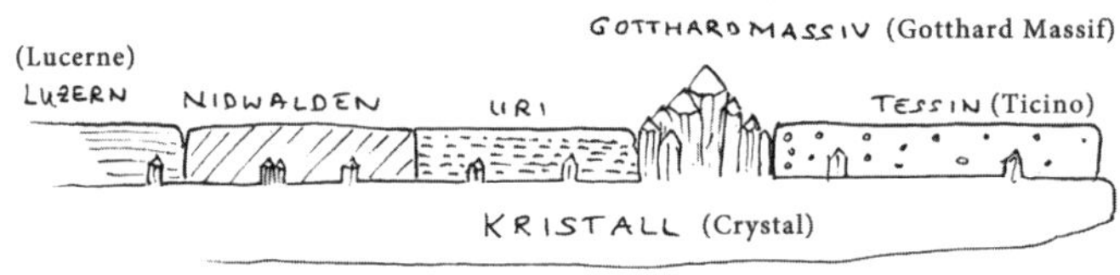

Fig. 12: Cross-section: Lucerne-Lugano.

This is how I saw Switzerland from above: On each cantonal stone there is a key, although each one has a different shape and a different style. It reflects something of the cultural distinctiveness of each canton. But it is always a key. The one for Geneva is a hotel key made of plastic. The bit points across the national border, as do the keys for Basle and Schaffhausen. None of the other key bits does this. The key for Zurich is the key to the Fraumünster church. It is made of brass. The key for Uri is an old church key. A canton in central Switzerland (Obwalden ?) is a simple, solid reservoir key. The key for Zug is in the form of a fish. The key for Aargau is a beautiful casket key. Its handle is in Brugg and its bit points to the Rhine. The key for Basle is a key with two separate bits, both of them pointing across the border, and behind the key can be seen the chemical formulae that belong to the key. The key for Schaffhausen is a modern, technical key, the bit pointing across the border. The key for Appenzell is a carved wooden bar. The key for St. Gallen is half-moon shaped and half-circular. The key for Glarus is probably an access key to an underground gallery. The key for Bern is a heavy unwieldy one. The key for the Jura is a cheese-cellar key. The key for Neuenburg is a factory key. The key for Freiburg is a key to a stable door, although it is almost too pretty for a stable door. The Vaud key is a neat

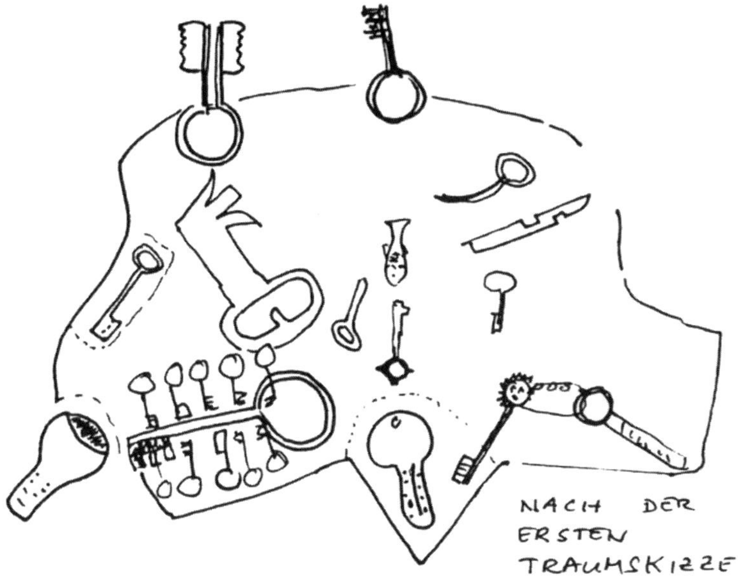

Fig. 13: As in the first dream sketch.

and pretty hand-made wooden dish. The Wallis has some 10-15 small chapel keys in the foreground with the bit pointing to the Rhone and at the back, one single large key, the handle in the Upper Wallis, the bit pointing to the Lower Wallis. The key for the Tessin is a Kaba security key as if for a safe. The key for the Grisons has a valley-bit it with a spiked mace handle, and on the same handle a finely engraved bit pointing to the Münstertal. I can't remember the shapes of the other cantonal keys.

But the keys, unlike the stones, are not connected to each other. The thought running through my head when I look at this puzzle more closely is that I would need a ring for all these keys to hold them together. This collection of keys reminds me of a painting by the gatekeeper of an old monastery where keys for every possible purpose were also kept together: for the church, the stables, workshops, kitchens, cells, stores etc. Anyone who is in charge of the keys would be in possession of such a collection of keys.

The Swiss woman sees Switzerland in the form of a puzzle. She is given something in which we can see a symbolic image of our state system. To get a better understanding of this impressive dream, we must first go back to the individual dream images again, looking at them from various angles and amplifying them. As it is such a long dream, we shall divide it up into sections.

From someone unknown to me I receive a sort of three-dimensional puzzle made of stones and keys which together make up the outline of Switzerland and correspond in number to our cantons. Each canton is made out of a stone which, of course, is shaped like its outline. And although the stones are all different, visually they form a whole.

The first part of the dream shows how our country is made up of very different cantonal stones. Despite this variety, the dream says that *visually they form a whole.* To enable us to have a better understanding of the symbolism of the stones, we must remind ourselves that each stone is simply how it is, and is there where it is. That is why in various cultures of the world, the essential, the unique and the unchangeable in man is seen as a stone. In that sense, a gravestone is a symbol of the immortal uniqueness of the human soul. And the alchemists' stone of wisdom was a symbol of the stable, established personality. Here in the dream, the individual cantonal stone represents the essential and distinctive aspects of the individual cantons.

As with an Asiatic puzzle, there is an end stone, and if this one stone is missing, the whole thing collapses. This key to the puzzle is a splendid, naturally formed, pyramid-like rock crystal in the shape of a key. It replaces the Gotthard Massif. Instead of the bit, this Gotthard-key-crystal has small crystals which link together from below in the cantonal stones, so that all the cantons are attached to each other and kept together. If it were not for the Gotthard-crystal-keystone, the cantonal stones would fall apart because they would not be connected to each other.

The individual cantons are held together by one single keystone without which everything would fall apart. As the dream says, it is a splendid, naturally formed, pyramid-like rock crystal in the shape of a key. Just as in the second part of the dream, in which each canton has its own key, this rock crystal is evidently the key to the cohesion of the whole Confederation and symbolises its very foundations.

A key can be used for opening or closing. It is that decisive "certain something" that can create connection but also demarcation. In the sphere of human coexistence, too, we use the image of the key. We need the right key to be able to approach certain people or to open up the heart of a loved one. That is why in the social sphere, the key is a symbol for what can reconcile and unite opposites but can also exclude anything that should not be there. It is therefore a symbol of love, for the key of love creates connection and therefore connectedness. At the same time, it also means limitation, demarcation, otherwise the love is not binding.

According to the dream, there is apparently a key that links all the cantons in Switzerland without detracting from the distinctiveness of each individual canton. Let us now take a look at what it is that makes this keystone so special. According to the dream, the key that connects the Confederation is actually something wonderful. It has grown in a natural way. Thus the thing that holds our country together deep down inside – the very heart of Switzerland – is a rock crystal that has gradually taken shape and, starting from the Gotthard, links the cantons together from below. Viewed in this light, the Confederation is not *an association that exists just for a specific purpose*, only to be dissolved when the benefits of coexistence are no longer clear.

So what is the meaning of the pyramid-shaped rock crystal which, according to the dream, replaces the Gotthard Massif? This pyramid form creates a meaningful link to the Pharaonic pyramids or to the gilded pyramid stone at the top of these pyramids or an obelisk. As a manifestation of the divine and the immortal aspects of the individual Pharaoh on earth, these constructions caught the first rays of the rising sun, symbol of the renewed, rejuvenated Sungod which the deceased Pharaoh has become. Consequently, the pyramid of the Gotthard crystal can be seen as connected to the key of Switzerland with a consciousness that is constantly being renewed.

The Gotthard key has a connection to the whole country. Remove it and everything falls apart. This crystal is the inner secret of what holds Switzerland together. We were introduced to the symbol of the rock crystal in the dream about the water samples (p. 39). As stated there, people used to

Fig.14: Solitaire of giant crystals discovered in the Gotthard region. This crystal is estimated to be 18 million years old.

think that crystals were made up of solidly frozen water in the depths of the earth (Greek: *crystallos* = ice). Thus in some way, this Gotthard crystal is related in meaning to the water of the Gotthard Massif. That would mean that all the things that have developed out of the symbol-creating ability of the Swiss collective soul, our myths and our symbolic values, ultimately form what holds our country together deep down inside. In the clear, transparent crystal, we find geometrical-mathematical structures as an expression of something spiritual on the one hand, and on the other hand, it consists of concrete matter. It is thus a union of spirit and matter and is therefore also a symbol of the union of opposites. Such symbols are always formed from the tolerating of apparently irreconcilable opposites. The essence, the basis of our State system would thus be what was gradually able to crystallise out of the juxtaposing of opposites in our country, be it the tension of opposites of town and country, city dweller and peasant, mountain and valley, right-wing and left-wing politics or, as we saw earlier, progress and tradition. As the "precious stone of the Swiss mountains", thanks to which the various classes, cultural and language groups are held together, *the Gotthard crystal stands as a symbol of the gradually crystallised mind and mentality of our country.*

In the preface to the Swiss Constitution, it says: «In the name of the Almighty.» Seen in this light, the Gotthard crystal could literally be understood as a symbol for the Almighty in the supra-denominational and thus superordinate sense. What is new about this symbol is that it represents, as already stated, a union of spirit and matter. If this orientation towards such a superordinate holistic entity were lost, then, as we can infer from the dream image, the very meaning of the existence of our federal system falls apart, and we would wear each other down in pursuing our private interests and priorities.

On each cantonal stone there is a key, although each one has a different shape and a different style. It reflects something of the cultural distinctiveness of each canton. But it is always a key.

The bridge to the second part of the dream, with the individual cantonal keys lying on the cantonal stones, is formed by the Gotthard rock crystal. For it is a stone on one side and a key on the other. The stone embodies rather the *stationary-passive* aspect of an individual entity, whereas the key represents more its *active* aspect. The Gotthard crystal, as both stone and key, also unites these opposites within itself. That is why it is in a position to hold all the parts together. It is a symbol of wholeness or – to phrase it in psychological terms – it is a *supradenominational image of God.*

Each canton consists of a stone and has its own distinctive key, so once again represents a centre of its own. The Confederation is depicted in the dream as a multiple entity, with a main centre (the Gotthard) and several secondary centres. That reflects the structure of the self, of the centring archetype that makes its presence felt in the collective of the land of the Swiss. And that corresponds to the archetype that is at the basis of democracy: every individual has his own life that is unique to him and at the same time builds a unified entity with others. And so every canton has its own key that holds together the unique inner essence of the individual cantons; this finds expression particularly well in the example of the canton of Wallis, where the one Wallis key connects the individual side-valley key(s). It is also nice to see how in this puzzle, the new canton of Jura is also represented as an individual entity.[59]

But the keys, unlike the stones, are not connected to each other. The thought running through my head when I look at this puzzle more closely is that I would need a ring for all these keys to hold them together. This collection of keys reminds me of a painting by the gatekeeper of an old monastery where keys for every possible purpose were also kept together: for the church, the stables, workshops, kitchens, cells stores etc. Anyone who is in charge of the keys would be in possession of such a collection of keys.

The problem now appears to be that unlike the cantonal stones, the cantonal keys are not linked to each other. According to the dream, there is a ring missing that could unite the keys. If we regard the keys as a symbol of the unique 'key power' of the individual cantons, then this ring signifies something that can be seen and thus experienced as a connecting factor that could again link together the interests of the individual cantons. According to the dream, the confederation of the individual cantons, "the collection of keys", seems to be in *need of reform*.

The dreamer's association with the collection of keys of a gatekeeper at a monastery is significant. For in a monastery, too, various interests (agriculture, craftsmanship, library etc.) are subordinate to God or a superordinate whole. What is missing in Switzerland today is a similar connecting and unifying element, like a ring, that could visibly link together the individual cantons in the day world. It is true, as we have seen, that on paper we have the Preface to our Federal Constitution «In the Name of the Almighty», but for many people today this introduction sounds superfluous and old-fashioned. This emerged very clearly in the detailed discussion in the federal Parliament about the preface to the new federal constitution.

Consequently even the older generation of Swiss sometimes find it difficult to say what actually links them to their fellow-countrymen, apart from the red passport. For they cannot give language, religion or geography

59 In 1978, in a federal plebiscite, the Jura was recognised as an independent canton. This brought a democratic conclusion to a conflict that dated back to the Congress of Vienna of 1814/15.

as a reason. And so people talk about the myth of Switzerland as *a nation that exists because it chooses to*, in other words, unlike other nations, it can justify its existence thanks to the political will of its people. The logical conclusion of this – and there is an element of risk involved – is that when the citizens have had enough of this nation, they can simply dissolve it.

The Swiss Confederation has lasted for 700 years because there has been a constant renewal or reform of the consciously experienced *sense of federation.* The initial union of the three original cantons meant something to everybody. This was evident whenever there was a threat from outside, and was reinforced by a shared trust in God. And on each occasion when the alliance was extended or renewed, this spirit prevailed. But every so often there were crises which almost led to the Confederation falling apart. What the image in the dream is telling us is that every time a crisis was overcome, the Gotthard crystal grew larger, and on the surface there was a reform or extension of the Confederation. That would correspond to the ring linking the different keys together. A new visible and almost tangible sense of existence was born which became a unifying force. That was the case, for example, with the Treaty of Stans in 1481,[60] or later, in 1848, when the federation became a federal state, and between 1933 and 1945 in the resistance against the Third Reich.

In the run-up to the celebrations for the 700th anniversary of the founding of Switzerland in 1991, and even more so in the voting on a possible entry into the European Economic Area in 1992, Swiss people once again experienced a fundamental identity crisis that is still clearly felt today on a political level. And so it seemed right and proper – and that is still the case today – to keep a sharp eye open for images in the depths of the unconscious which could contribute to a deeper understanding of what lies behind this *crisis of unity*. On December 12, 1990, as I was working on the interpretation of the Dream about the Gotthard crystal, I had the following dream, which seemed very relevant. It has been shortened here.

60 The Treaty of Stans of 1481 marked an end to the latent conflict between the 8 rural and urban cantons of the old Swiss Confederacy. As a result, it had expanded to 13 cantons by 1513. See "Stanser Verkommnis", written by E. Walder in: *Historisches Lexikon der Schweiz in 13 Bänden*, Vol. 11, Basle 2012.

No. 31, Dream about the well in a Swiss village:

I am with a woman / my wife in a village that is falling into ruin and which is actually Switzerland. The wood on the houses, which in themselves are very pretty, and the wooden well, carved out of a tree trunk, are rotting because the water is not being drained away properly. There may well be drainpipes on the roof but it is all marshy swamp where the well is. [...] The well itself needs further care and attention since it has not been cleaned out for a long time, as would be necessary for such a large and lovely wooden well. The place is heavily polluted by the large numbers of serpents and vermin which are able to thrive and reproduce in abundance in this swampy marshland.

Then a rainbow-coloured, worm-like serpent comes towards us. It is a short, phallus-like serpent and moves incredibly quickly. The animal is the king of the serpents. At first I am tempted to flee, but the woman, my wife, laughs and says that she knows this serpent, and indeed she treats it with great affection. And so I gain its confidence and it also comes to me. The serpent shows me that she loves me, too, and I no longer feel the need to run away (as in the legend motif of the serpent kiss).

Then the serpent disappears into a classroom of the Arabic-English Translation Department of the American University of Cairo.

The dream shows clearly that there is something seriously wrong at the very heart of the Swiss village, the symbol of our identity. The problem lies in the fact that firstly, the rainwater is not being collectively drained away from the houses and secondly, the groundwater is not kept clean in the fountain because the fountain itself has not been kept clean. We need to look at these two problems separately.

The new drainpipes on the individual houses in the Swiss village indicate that a diverting of the rainfall is a symbol of *what flows to Man from the other world*, in other words, a renewal of the collecting and diverting of the water from the unconscious is regarded as something that is necessary and will be carried out, even if it is only on one's own private rooftop. This could be understood to mean that in the sphere of the individual or of small groups, it has been recognised that there is a need for either a passing on of the contents coming up from the unconscious or protection against them. On the other hand, the new drainpipes, without any further outlet for the water, can be understood as a graphic expression of the fact that in the Swiss village, the collecting and the diverting of water, i.e. the careful attention given to the water from the unconscious *is no longer a community issue*.

At community level, this collective diverting was the original function of the religious orders. Once they lost their sense of creating a community spirit, it was "as if the individual houses had retreated into themselves": religion, or the connection to the non-rational, the unconscious, has become a matter for the individual or small groups. What is apparently missing in the Swiss village is a *supra-denominational "collecting and passing on" of the unconscious contents* as represented in the dream image.

This is in contrast to earlier times when the "village church" represented a common focal point of religious life. As is now emerging more and more clearly, the Christian attitude to life also has its one-sided aspects. What is lacking in patriarchal Christianity is satisfactory answers to such questions as the feminine, matter, nature, sexuality, but also the problem of the reality of evil, as we have seen earlier. To compensate for these one-sided elements of the Christian faith, so-called *story circles* were set up in rural areas, in some areas even up to the beginning of the last century, in which consideration was given to such matters as the legendary, the inexplicable and the uncanny. The result was that numinous incidents and experiences, which burst the boundaries of the Christian context, could be apprehended and taken note of in group discussions.[61] Both the Christian world image with its symbols, together with non-Christian symbols, made it possible for tradition-bound people to have a *shared involvement with symbolic life*. And this made it possible for the contents of the other world, from the unconscious, to be integrated into the conscious life of the community, so that life could continue to "flow on", so to speak, remaining in the image of the dream.

Today, by way of contrast, there is a danger that the world of consciousness may turn into a marshy swamp. Let us look, for example, at the parallel worlds of the sexual underworld, where sexuality with no sense of relatedness

61 See for example: G. Isler, *Die Sennenpuppe. Eine Untersuchung über die religiöse Funktion von einigen Alpensagen.* Schriften der schw. Gesellschaft für Volkskunde Vol. 52, Basle 1971. And by the same author: *Lumen naturae,* Egg 2000.

Fig. 15 Wooden trough.

has become meaningless and hence perverted, or at the increasingly widespread and compulsive acquisitive greed to go out and buy. The slogan these days in the Swiss village is: "*anything goes*". If the symbolic contents of the influences and drives from the unconscious are not grasped and understood, they stem the very flow of life so that it mingles with terrestrial soil, a symbol of physical reality. The result, as stated, is an unhealthy and dangerous quagmire in which all sorts of serpents and vermin are able to thrive and multiply. The latter are a symbol for a collective psychic dissociation, a fragmentation, for example, into the aforementioned various emotional drives or, on the external level, into political side issues and details. When this happens, the two main problems in the dream – the need for this swamp to be cleaned up and the significance of a clean well – are no longer acknowledged. If the swamp is to be cleaned up and allowed to dry out, there is obviously first of all an urgent need for a proper common outlet. Time will tell how this problem is effectively solved. The immediate priority is *the acknowledging of the problem.*

A central feature of the Swiss village in the dream is a large, beautiful wooden well, carved out of a tree trunk. Such wells can still be found in some mountain villages and alpine pastures (Fig. 15). But in the dream, the well is unusable, surrounded as it is by a quagmire and not having been cleaned for a long time. And so it is rotting away. It therefore seems particularly important that due attention be given to the symbolism of fountains. At this point, I should like to refer to some reflections from Chinese culture which, in wonderful poetry, help us to understand what essentially lies behind this symbolism. In the *I Ching, the Chinese Book of Changes*, there is a chapter dedicated to wells and in particular to the restoration of a well that is no longer usable. This is a significant problem that crops up in the dream and needs to be dealt with accordingly. Under the Change sign No. 48, we read the following:

> *THE WELL.*
> *The town may be changed,*
> *But the well cannot be changed.*
> *It neither decreases nor increases.*
> *They come and go and draw from the well.*

If one gets down almost to the water
And the rope does not go all the way,
Or the jug breaks,
It brings misfortune.[62]

The commentary to these initially somewhat puzzling lines runs as follows:

«In ancient China, the capital cities were sometimes moved, partly for the sake of a more favourable location, partly because of a change in dynasties. The style of architecture changed in the course of centuries, but the shape of the well has remained the same from ancient times to this day. Thus the well is the symbol of that social structure which, evolved by mankind in meeting its most primitive needs, is independent of all political forms. Political structures change, as do nations, but the life of man with its needs remains eternally the same; this cannot be changed. Life is also inexhaustible. It grows neither less nor more; it exists for one and for all. The generations come and go, and all enjoy life in its inexhaustible abundance.»

Each of the 64 change symbols in the I Ching consists of six unbroken or broken lines, so-called Lines of Change. This is what the change symbol No. 48 looks like:

For each of these six Lines of Change there is a text, together with a commentary, relating to the state or the restoration of the well. The state of

62 Quoted from the I Ching – *The Book of Changes*, The Richard Wilhelm translation rendered into English by Cary F. Baynes. New York 1952; p. 197-198.

the "Swiss well" in the dream is described in relation to the bottom Line of Change of the symbol No. 48 in the I Ching. The corresponding text is:

One does not drink the mud of the well.
No animals come to an old well.

The relevant commentary: «If a man wanders around in the swampy lowlands, his life is submerged in the mud. Such a man loses all significance for mankind. He who throws himself away is no longer sought out by others. In the end no one troubles about him anymore.»[63]

Here we have a description of the effect a neglected well has on an individual person. Anyone who fails to cultivate the connection to the inner life water and thus, so to speak, "throws himself away", forfeits his significance for mankind. But this dream applies to the collective, not just an individual. The village is a symbol for the whole of Switzerland, and the state of the well must thus correspond to the state described in the I Ching.

As Hans Giger states in the book we have already referred to, *Die verlorene Ehre der Helvetia* (The Lost Honour of Helvetia), Switzerland, in political terms, is on the point of giving up the State that it has nurtured and developed, its own political structures and fabric and its very identity. It seems to have adopted a willingness to make concessions, to be less determined to impose limitations.[64] There is a serious danger that Switzerland, in the words of the I Ching, may ultimately be "throwing itself away" and thereby losing its significance for other countries. In recent times, we have paid less attention to the life-giving symbols of the depths, which are what provide a country with the constant renewal of its life force.

The other five Lines of Change in No. 48 in the I Ching emphasise (from bottom to top) the restoration of the well. The text for the top Line of Change, after the work has been completed is:

63 I Ging, p. 199.

64 Hans Giger, *Die verlorene Ehre der Mutter Helvetia, Politische Machtentfaltung im Fokus allgemeiner Rechtsprinzipien,* Zurich 2012. Here, the lawyer and professor Hans Giger, describes how there is a risk that executive, legislative and jurisdiction might destroy the basis of legislation and disempower the Swiss people. He sees this danger in the concentration of the powers of these institutions, together with the misuse of power by politicians and the way they seek the limelight, supported by the media, as a fourth power, which play an important part by taking sides.

One draws from the well without hindrance.
It is dependable. Supreme good fortune.

The commentary says: «The well is there for all. No one is forbidden to take water from it. No matter how many come, all find what they need, for the well is dependable. It has a spring and never runs dry. Therefore it is a great blessing to the whole land. The same is true of the really great man, whose inner wealth is inexhaustible; the more that people draw from him, the greater his wealth becomes.»

Of great importance is what it says in the commentary to the whole Changes diagram: «.... [F]or a satisfactory political or social organisation of mankind ... [we] must go down to the very foundations of life. For any merely superficial ordering of life that leaves its deepest needs unsatisfied is as ineffectual as if no attempt at order had ever been made.» The dream image of the place *where the well is located* seems to be pointing out the same thing, since it stands in *marshy swamp.* The restoration of the water diversion and the well in the Swiss village must be tackled very thoroughly. Any superficial cosmetic work is a waste of time. That is also indicated in the second part of the dream, which now follows.

Then a rainbow-coloured, worm-like serpent comes towards us. It is a short phallus-like serpent and moves incredibly quickly. The animal is the king of the serpents.

Clearly the animal wishes to be noticed, for in the dream, it approaches us directly. As a so-called "royal animal", it indicates the possibility of finding unity amid the dissociation of so many animals, since the king symbolism points to a bringing together of elements in a situation where there is divergence. What is particularly striking is the worm-like shape of the animal. As C.G. Jung showed in his work *Mysterium coniunctionis*, the worm-shaped serpent can represent a surprising change in form of the supreme value of a society, the notion of God, the image of God.[65]

65 C.G. Jung; *Mysterium coniunctionis, Coll. Works* 14.II, part IV: Rex and Regina, chapter "The dark side of the king", p. 336ff (§474 ff).

As Christianity has never dealt satisfactorily with the issues of the divinity of matter, nature, the human body and sexuality, the Christian God image has lost its effectiveness for many people. When the general conception of the divine, the image of God ages – when a church that has grown tired is no longer a force in the village – it sinks down into the underworld, into the unconscious. There the experience of God lives on as a phallus-like serpent or a worm to rise again in altered form as a renewed uniter of opposites.

The fact that the serpent displays the colours of the rainbow shows that it is a life spirit. The rainbow, in all its colours, symbolises in the Bible God's promise and sign of alliance towards Noah and mankind. God promised never again to cause such destruction as that brought on by the Flood (1.Moses, 9-17). Viewed thus, the rainbow symbolises new life. Accordingly, the rainbow serpent can be understood as a spirit of renewal in nature that is linked to life. Given this numinous aspect (of the serpent), it comes as no surprise that the dreamer is filled with alarm.

Finally the serpent disappears into a classroom of the Arabic-English Translation Department of the American University of Cairo. For me, the Arabic Language and Cairo are associated with Arabic alchemy because I learned Arabic so as to be able – together with a translator in Cairo – to translate manuscripts on Arabic alchemy. As C.G. Jung showed, the over 2000-year-old tradition of symbolic alchemy had nothing to do with making gold; it was rather the attempt to reconcile the laws of nature, the God image of the philosophers of nature and the scientists, with the Islamic and also the Christian God image and to create a permanent link between them. So, if the phallus-shaped serpent disappears off to Egypt, it can be assumed that it is the place where creative, in-depth work can be accomplished. Evidently we must continue our efforts to deal more comprehensively with the growing conflict between religion and science.[66]

The following dream reveals to what depths the question of national defence can lead. It comes from a young scientist who, at the time, was heavily involved with the qualitative aspect of natural numbers but gave no thought at all to the subject of national defence. He had the dream on August 10, 1984.

66 Initial results of this translation work are to be found in the *Corpus Alchemicum Arabicum* (CALA) published by Th. Abt and W. Madelung. Zurich 2001 f.

No. 32, Dream about the Depth Research Centre:

I am in the place where I attended kindergarten. That is where the entrance is to an ultra-modern Depth Research Centre of incredible depth: over 2000 metres down into the earth. The Centre is of supreme importance for our national defence. Somehow I managed to gain entrance and, with the aid of a special lift, came into the Centre, from which corridors led off in all directions in the shape of a star. What amazed me most was the fact that the difference in pressure from the surface was automatically regulated in the lift so that I also felt quite well down below. Back on top, I entered my parents' house, which was now my house. There I talked a little about my experience.

There is evidently a "subterranean corridor system" that is of great importance for the defence of Swiss independence, as it says in the dream. At a depth of 2000 metres in the external world, it is hardly likely that tunnels have been built, so the dream statement must be regarded as symbolic. The subterranean tunnel system, arranged in the shape of a star, points to an already existing centred basic structure in the depths of this country. We can view it as a symbol of a deeper-lying wholeness. The dream tells us that there exists – by means of a lift – the possibility to descend to these depths once again and establish a relationship with this sphere.

As mentioned earlier, the dreamer was preoccupied at the time with the qualitative aspect of the number. That belongs to the field of basic mathematical research. All exact sciences are formulated mathematically today; even in Psychology, attempts are made to establish connections via statistics. For a long time, it was held to be *the* certain foundation. However, since Kurt Gödel[67] proved in 1931 that natural numbers are logical *and* illogical, it may be deduced that this also applies to the fundamentals of mathematics and ultimately to our conception of the world image.[68]

67 Kurt Gödel (1906-1978) was an Austrian-American mathematician and one of the most important logicians of the 20th century. An introduction to his ideas can be found in Douglas R. Hofstadter: *Gödel, Escher, Bach. An eternal golden braid.* New York 1979.

68 M.-L. von Franz, *Number and Time: Reflections Leading Toward a Unification of Depth Psychology and Physics.* Evanston, Ill. 1986, p. 28-30.

The huge split that is also shaking the foundations of our State today is the one that exists between the allegedly exact sciences such as Physics on the one hand and Religion on the other. As was hinted at in the previous dream about the Swiss village, the task facing us today is to work on bridging this split. For today, many people are yearning for a comprehensive, all-embracing understanding of the world, in which both the rational and the (hitherto irreconcilable) extra-rational approach to reality are linked together in a way that will bear fruit and prosper. According to the dream, the expanding of the understanding of the fundamentals of mathematics is what points the way, as we shall see in what follows.[69]

In the dream, special mention is made of the great difference in pressure between the world at the top and 2000 metres below ground

What amazed me most was the fact that the difference in pressure from the surface was automatically regulated in the lift so that I also felt quite well down below. Back on top, I entered my parents' house, which was now my house. There I talked a little about my experience.

Public life is played out on the surface of the earth, whereas the healing powers – the healing water from the dream about the water samples – are to be found in the psychological depths. The dream tells us that there is a great difference in pressure between the world above and the world below, but this difference is "automatically regulated" so the dreamer still feels well. This may be interpreted as an indication that the path to deep introversion has certainly become feasible, the way having been paved through an enormous cultural achievement of our forefathers. We can understand this if we bear in mind the ascetic-introverted basic attitude of the Swiss, who, with the limitations imposed by Nature, were virtually obliged to develop in a deeper rather than a broader way.

With these insights from the depths of the *ultra-modern Depth Research Centre*, the dreamer returned to the parental home, which in the dream became his home. This would be an image for a happy connection between the knowledge acquired from the depths and that of the upper world

69 L.c., p. 27-28.

day consciousness. The use of the adjective highly modern emphasises just how up-to-date this knowledge is.

Down below in the depths, a star-shaped foundation for the national defence is already in place. This shows that when one 'goes into' introversion, and allows oneself to be transported into the inner depths, then everything is there that is needed to gain a better understanding of the situation up above and to provide possible healing. According to the dream, one must simply have the confidence to turn to these depths. It is there, in the depths of the unconscious, that the secret of the ability to defend Swiss independence lies hidden. This book demonstrates that crucial insights concerning the defence of our independence and the very meaning of the existence of Switzerland are to be found in the unconscious.

13. In the name of the Almighty

The question of national defence on a mental level led us to the question of the basis of the Swiss state system and further into the depths of the religious problems of our time. The following dream from a 35-year-old Swiss, which occurred on July 6, 1982, reveals another aspect of the problem that is worthy of consideration:

No. 33, Dream about the audible prayer:

Someone (the deity himself?) tells me that there is a huge difference in whether a community worships God individually and in silence or whether a prayer can also be heard outside. For the latter joins people together, like the Betruf (prayer call of the herdsman)[70] *in the Swiss mountains.*

The dream actually speaks for itself. It shows that there is a difference whether or not, in a society, there is a wholeness or entity superordinate to man that used to be called God, and is commonly recognised and revered.

As we know, this common and public recognition and reverence for the deity is crumbling, and not only in Switzerland. When the revision of the Federal Constitution was on the agenda, there was a discussion as to whether or not the preface «In the Name of the Almighty» should be retained in the new version. In most of the cantonal constitutions, this preface has in the meantime been formulated in different ways such as: «[...] with a sense of responsibility towards Creation [...]» (Bern, 1993); or «conscious of our responsibility to God, and to our fellowmen and nature [...]» (Grisons, 2003); or «[...] with a sense of responsibility towards Creation and in the knowledge of the limitations of human power [...]» (Zurich, 2005); or «[...] in the awareness that the responsibility towards future generations calls for a sustainable and human attitude to nature and an application of human knowledge that respects man and the environment [...]» (Tessin 206); or «[...] with a sense

70 The prayer call is a sort of ritual prayer carried out by the herdsman to protect his alp that is communicated to his animals and neighbours.

of responsibility before God to our fellowmen and nature [...]» (Lucerne, 2007); or «[...] which regards Creation as the cradle of future generations, is open to the world and feels connected with it [...]» (Vaud, 2012). This shows that in Switzerland we can no longer easily agree on what the superordinate wholeness or entity should be called. This situation is the expression of a change in values, specifically the supreme value in society: the image of God. For some 1500 years, the image of God in Europe was shaped by Christianity, by a masculine Trinity, but since the Enlightenment, this has changed and developed into something different: Creation, nature, man and matter. And all this finds expression in the various cantonal constitutions above.

So what counts now: the Almighty or Creation, nature, matter? We cannot answer this question with an "either / or". For both of them contain a centring divine force: the values of Christianity, expressed by tradition *in the Name of the Almighty*, as well as the values of the Enlightenment, made visible, as it were, *in the name of Creation, nature and matter*, and thus in the name of past, present and future generations. Both have become supreme values: for some it is the first area that counts as the supreme value, for others it is more the second. This makes it clear that there is a need for a reconciling of these opposites of a Christian Trinity and a material world that is not contained in this conception of God.[71] For when the majority of people in a society cannot be guided by a united superordinate force, there is a danger that the differing conceptions of what the supreme value is can destroy the elements that bind a society together. An example of this is Hyderabad (India), where the rival religious communities of Hindus and Muslims try to outdo each other with ever louder muezzin prayers and temple chants. That can hardly be what is meant by «prayers audible outside». The other extreme is the possibility expressed in the dream that the deity is revered individually and in silence and the prayer cannot be heard outside. In the dream, we learn that

there is a huge difference in whether a community worships God individually and in silence or whether a prayer can also be heard outside. For the latter joins people together, like the Betruf (prayer call) in the Swiss mountains.

71 See in detail Th. Abt "Forschung am Wendepunkt", in *Landwirtschaft Schweiz*, 3/5 (1990), p. 259-265.

Fig. 16: Prayer call of the mountain herdsman in Inner Appenzell. Photography: Cyrill Schläpfer 1990.

According to the dream, a retreat from a purely personal connection with the divine, preferred by many, is apparently no solution. With the prayer call as night falls on the Alpine pasture, a single dairyman takes over the function of the priest and calls in all four directions for a blessing so that the Alp be protected from the so-called 'It' with the ritual of the symbolic golden ring. In this 'It', we recognise the unconscious, with its unpredictable powers, which must be opposed during the night by the protective ring of consciousness (gold). The tradition of the prayer call of the mountain herdsman in Switzerland has been kept alive despite earlier protests from the Church. It is an audible expression of a very meaningful ritual on the part of dairymen and the Alpine community. Symbolically it represents on the one hand a link within the ring and thus creates trust and confidence; on the other hand, the ring establishes a protective barrier against what lies outside it. But if people are no longer bound in such a way to something that is a *common superordinate concept*, then selfishness, lies and intrigue can become widespread and the notion of might is right asserts itself.

As could be seen in the colourful collection of prefaces to cantonal constitutions, words alone are not really capable of expressing and creating a feeling of unity. Only *a living symbol* can build a bridge to the other side, to the superordinate whole, and that has always been so. A case in point is the enormous binding power of the symbol of the cross at the time of the transition from the Western Roman Empire to the Eastern Roman Empire (New Rome), later named Constantinople. The Christianisation of the Roman Empire was the consequence of a dream of Emperor Constantine: «[…] at some point before the Battle of the Milvian bridge (312), he and his army saw in the heavens a cross of light above the sun, carrying the message *en touto nika* or "with this [sign], you will conquer". Constantine did not understand this sign for a long time; but he had a dream the night before the battle, in which Christ appeared with the same heavenly sign, and told him to make a standard for his army in that form. The main standard of the army was accordingly decorated with a Christogram.»[72] It remains to be seen what symbol will bestow on Switzerland such reviving force, but the dream image of the Gotthard crystal gives us some idea of the mysterious effectiveness of a unifying symbol.

No doubt the common future of the Swiss will ultimately depend on whether there can be a revival of the experience of – and the relation to – the divine, which motivated our forefathers to write their preface to the Federal Constitution. That would mean that the basis of the federal state system would once again be experienced "in the name of the Almighty", that is to say with an appropriate sense of wholeness comprising consciousness and the unconscious. Expressed in contemporary language, that would mean that in living alongside each other, *we should be guided by the innermost depths of the collective unconscious and focus on essentials in a fundamentally new way.*

72 Written by Bishop Eusebius of Caesarea in *Vita Constantini* (1,27-32).

Part IV

Against the Surrendering of Identity

14. The danger of the surrendering of identity

The period after the fall of the Berlin Wall could be described as a "euphoria of peace". And still today in (Switzerland and) Europe, it is hard to imagine the threat of war. The EU having been awarded the Nobel Peace Prize, there are now hopes that within this framework it will be able to bring peace to other areas, the Balkans, for example. A veritable wave of confidence and relief could be felt, even though the nations of Europe are still living in the shadow of huge potential destruction.

Some twenty years ago, around the time of the vote on the abolition of the Swiss Army, a survey was conducted of archetypal dreams; some of those dreams are presented in this book. The chapters "The Seriousness of the Situation" and "Camouflaging the Threat" in Part II showed that in contrast to the general mood of joy at the end of the Cold War, a feeling of being under threat was starting to manifest itself in the unconscious. In Part III, an earlier dream on the subject of the defence of Swiss independence, with the image of poisonous gas, revealed evidence of an insidious ideological poisoning that had long been imperceptible. It showed clearly how the strength of the idea of a permanently united and peaceful Europe could make possible a gradual weakening of Swiss independence. But the basic features of Parts II and III demonstrated not only how Swiss independence might be jeopardised but also, with impressive symbols, such as that of the Gotthard crystal, showed the value and meaning of an independent Switzerland, as well as elements of a possible guiding principle for the future.

In former times, the Confederation was threatened by clearly recognisable external powers or internal conflicting interests. Today – according to the dreams – we are faced rather with a diffuse psychological threat that goes by the name of the surrendering of identity. Back in the 1990s, especially among a large section of the younger generation, it was felt to be necessary that the Helvetic system should be opened up and fundamentally changed. On the political level at that time, this diffuse threat to the Swiss identity had not gone unrecognised, and as a result, quite a few possible measures were put forward for discussion. In the spring of 1991, the then Liberal State councillor, René Rhinow, had complained to the Federal Council about the debilitating lack of faith in our State system and demanded that it be replaced by a new set of values and objectives, and that the image of what is *wrong* with Switzerland should be replaced by one of what is *right* about Switzerland.[73] He found support for his views from the Lower Chamber. The character, the very essence of Helvetia, was thus under critical examination not just in progressive circles but in liberal circles as well. Since then, visions, hopes and wishes about the future of Switzerland have been published by various well-known figures. All of this goes to prove that *there is a definite need in Switzerland for the restoration of a sense and feeling of belonging together.*

The crisis in the Confederation's conception of itself was also reflected in the increasing institutional connection to the EU. Thus quite a few people in Switzerland seem to have come to regard it as impossible for the country to continue to exist as an independent country in Europe. Seen in this light, it could well be that the next decisive fight of the Swiss Army will not be against an external enemy but against an internal psychological one – *the surrendering of identity.*

The difficult thing in dealing with this insidious threat of the surrendering of identity is the fact that non-rational and partially unconscious factors are involved. For this reason, we shall here in Part IV shed more light on which driving forces are undermining this need for independence. The first step will be to examine – with regard to Europe – what hints we are receiving from the images of the depths of the soul that would help us to understand these enigmatic driving forces that render obsolete the need for an independent Switzerland and thus call into question the State system that is in place (Chap. 15). The second step would involve examining what can be done from the viewpoint of the unconscious to counter this paralysing surrendering of identity.

73 R. Rhinow, *Neue Zürcher Zeitung,* January 12/13th, 1991.

15. Switzerland and Europe from the viewpoint of the unconscious

The subject of the national identity of Switzerland is linked to the Europe question, but the question of identity also applies to other European countries, so let us first examine here what the unconscious has to say to Europe itself. Due to the compensatory response of the unconscious, dreams, as already stated, generally indicate things that one has not thought of on a conscious level.

We begin with a dream of a Swedish man, a 67-year-old businessman. Together with his wife, he was on the way to France by car, to look for a suitable place where they could then spend half of the year. Given the extremely high taxes in Sweden, they would thus be able to lead a much more comfortable life with their savings. That is what they had worked out. The sentimental value of being able to spend the autumn of their life in their own country could not outweigh the material benefit of the tax savings. When they were in Heidelberg on November 19th, in 1990, the man had a dream:

No. 34, Dream of the smelly beaver kiss:

Together with my family, I found myself in a pedestrian underpass in the vicinity of Stockholm. Suddenly a strange animal ran up to us with two of her young. The animal was beaver-like, but also reminiscent of a marmot. I knew that it would be a disaster for the ecological balance and the species diversity of the animal world if this species were to establish itself with us in Scandinavia, because it would immediately spread like wildfire. So I vigorously tried to fend off the animal by kicking and thumping it. But the mother, nimble and determined and completely ignoring my anger, jumped up like a dog and kissed me. The animal's breath reminded me of a decaying corpse. It was absolutely unbearable and left me almost paralysed. Then the animal jumped into a nearby puddle, rolled around in it and revelled in the long-awaited Promised Land. From there, the beast kept an eye on her young and looked at me with gleaming eyes which said: "Victory will be ours!"

We shall try to shed light on the meaning of this dream document with the aid of the amplification method. The setting of the action is an underpass back home in Sweden. Psychologically an underpass, which leads from one side to the other, is a symbol for a transition. As any psychological transition is also fraught with danger, people have always felt the protective need for so-called rites of passage.[74] For those still in employment, transition into the "third half of life" is also not entirely risk-free, for many people lose their sense of belonging, and life becomes less meaningful when they reach retirement age.

Something dangerous is evident in this dream in the form of an over-friendly yet determined and aggressive rodent. In dreams, animals embody the animal side of our nature, that is, our instincts. Thus an animal in our dreams shows us what driving force is at work, a force that we may not even be aware of. As the dreamer was on his way to France to look for a second home, thus surrendering a part of his identity, it is relevant to our question about the identity problem of Switzerland to examine what sort of animal is involved here.

As the animal in the dream is similar to the beaver, we must first of all take a closer look at the beaver itself. Beavers are decidedly intelligent and industrious rodents, which come together to form larger colonies. The Swedish man knew this. He knew also about the beaver's amazing ability to build fortresses and dams in groups, and to create new wetland habitats in his role of landscape designer. It is understandable why, for the natives of North America, the beaver is considered to have medicinal powers and cultural significance. The beaver, which forms groups to set up constructive communities and, by creating new habitats, has a beneficial effect on further biodiversity, would thus be a symbol for a positive creative driving force.

74 This term was coined by Arnold van Gennep 1909. Cf. Arnold van Gennep: *The Rites of Passage*. London 1960, French Original title: *Les Rites de passage*.

In this spirit, an amalgamation of individual entities into larger ones is creatively constructive.[75]

The animal in our dream, however, is not just similar to the beaver but is also reminiscent of the marmot. We must therefore familiarise ourselves with its distinctive characteristics. Known as Alpine inhabitants,

Fig. 17: A beaver construction.

[75] Amplifications about the beaver symbolism come from B. *Grzimek's Animal Life Encyclopedia. Vol 16, (Mammals)*, p. 177-184.

the socially-minded marmot, like the beaver, lives in colonies. Not infrequently they inhabit constructions of enormous proportions. They are also known to hibernate and to have a warning whistle when danger threatens, and like humans, they have the ability to stand upright. Like beavers, marmots are very attached to their own territory.

Unlike the real beaver or the real marmot, the animal in the dream is intrusively friendly in an unnatural way and seeks contact with the dreamer. This is a form of behaviour that we rarely see in wild animals, especially in a mother with her young. In addition, the animal has a strange, incredibly crafty aggressiveness and is confident of victory. These are clear indications of a behavioural disorder. The rotten carcass smell of its breath in the dream is indicative of a decaying process, something unwholesome and hostile to life, which weakens any attempt to put up resistance. In the dream, the animal, despite opposition, is able to plant a kiss, which shows that it has great determination.

At the end of the dream, the hybrid creature is fortunate to have reached its Promised Land in a puddle. The dreamer was raised as a Christian and the Promised Land was known to him as the land of milk and honey. This was the country into which Joshua had led the people of Israel. As the man himself was on a journey to find his own "Promised Land" in the sunny South, we recognise in the beaver-like animal an instinct which – in a somewhat inappropriate form – is looking for paradise in a puddle. This was the dream's comment on the dreamer's plan: something stinks here in the depths of the soul.

So first of all, the dream had something to say to the dreamer himself. Something on the following lines: look, you are getting involved with a rather too friendly, but nauseating, smelly, maladjusted animal which is seeking its paradise in the wrong place. Your desire to seek home and sense of community in a place where life is most comfortable and convenient stems from a dangerous drivenness which could upset the balance of your other animals, i.e. your entire instinctual basis. When the man told his wife about the dream, they both saw it as a bad omen and abandoned their plans.

So much for the personal meaning of the dream. But today, it is basically possible for people to settle anywhere in Europe, and the individual exploiting of this to the full has become a general guiding principle. As a result, the dream has a meaning that extends beyond the personal. It shows the image of a 'stink-friendly' animal. Psychologically, what might this animal mean that according to the dream is so intent on seeking the "Promised Land", and that multiplies so rapidly that it poses a threat to the ecological balance of biodiversity? The sentence at the end gives us a clue. The self-confident: "Victory will be ours!" reminded the Swede, whose father had been a soldier in the Second World War, of that aggressive expansionist nation which also for a time destroyed biodiversity, with its ideology of a unified "Greater Europe" under German leadership. Again and again at that time, the slogan "Victory will be ours." could be heard from the Reich propaganda department. Thus, the deviant animal probably symbolises something more general, something that can be observed in Europe today.

Lurking behind the enthusiasm to build a "United Europe", there might consequently be – so the dream is possibly suggesting – an insistent political force, one which does not respect boundaries and is no longer willing to respect the uniqueness and the distinctiveness of the other person with his attempts to actually establish those boundaries. The animal in the dream would therefore be the symbolic expression of a spirit of egalitarianism. It plants a kiss whether it is wished for or not. And with its foul breath it breaks down the resistance towards him in a rather diabolical way. Actually, there is something in Europe that lacks respect for barriers. When we see, for example, how inexorably general standards are enforced and how extremely difficult it is to resist this type of pressure to conform today, we feel that here there might be some unconscious collective driving force at work which can be detected in the symbol of this disgusting animal.

Basically this is correct: the Christian West has become old and weary and needs new models and values which could reconnect the countries of Europe on a higher level of consciousness. That would be the actual creative task which has become imperative in our 21st century. This calls for constructive images from the inner spiritual night world, the world of the beyond, from which every cultural revival has hitherto emerged. That would be the creative spirit of the beaver. But unlike the real beaver as a bringer of healing and culture, a "failed beaver" with smelly breath seems to be multiplying unchecked at the moment.

This is a sick demon, which aggressively and confidently strives to reach his "promised land" and might achieve this goal against all odds, thanks to his stinking and debilitating breath. The Greek word for breathing is *pneuma*, which also means spirit. This smelly breath would correspond to a 'natural poison gas', so to speak. This demon, which needs to be fought against in a timely and effective manner, could be a symbol of an *unsuccessful preliminary stage prior to a genuine and creative renewal.*

Unsuccessful attempts at creativity happen again and again during cultural crises. This problem can be observed in various creation myths, where the first attempts failed to bring the right creations into the world. The creator-spirit or the deity sought to create people in various myths, for example, but did not succeed at the first attempt. The first beings, such as the Titans in Greek mythology, were huge, destructive, idiotic or unable to move properly. At any rate, the whole thing was a failure, and so the creator had to destroy his creation again or tame it, and start all over again. Sometimes, there were several failed attempts, until finally the deity or the creator managed to produce something which was able to survive and exist.[76]

Viewed thus, there is much that might be learned from this dream. Behind the self-serving external search for the "promised land" with the ensuing material advantages, there stands a wrongly developed instinct that brings nothing constructive. Instead, this drive weakens and threatens people's sense of deep-rootedness. What is therefore essential is first of all the necessary moral force to withstand the approach of this deviant animal, in the way the Swedish man tried to do. Through individuals who have become aware of the drive potential of the limited personal maximisation of exploitability, a "real creative beaver power" could assert itself in a revival of our European cultural awareness. We see from this that the subject of identity loss is a *supranational* one.

The following dream shows how local identity in Switzerland may be destroyed through globalisation and profit-making mindedness. It comes from a 66-year-old social worker from Central Switzerland. She was very

76 For more detail, see M.-L. von Franz, *Patterns of Creativity mirrored in Creation Myths.* Zurich 1972. Chapter X: Abortive Attempts of Creation, p. 170-189. Viewed in this light, the development in Germany of the Hitler era can be regarded as a failed attempt at creative renewal. The same, with different preconditions, goes for the Hippie movement.

concerned about change and the future of Switzerland, and she had the following dream, slightly condensed here:

No. 35, Dream of the demolition of the brick building:

I'm in the canton of Glarus, in a sunny, rather narrow mountain valley. Left of us, an imposing brick building rises. Externally it seems rather dilapidated. You can see a woman bustling in and out. Someone says that this house will be demolished. Nothing more can be done to it. It upsets me to think that such a good building should yield to a soulless new one. Someone mentions that the house is to be replaced by an international-style hotel. I ask: Sheraton chain? We have no details. All we know is that the new management will turn the hotel into a profitable concern.

As I walk away, I see the building again in all its imposing grandeur: the beautiful brick building, almost reminiscent of the Baroque. At the rear, it also has attachments that look like greenhouses or low-rise service buildings. Everything is so friendly and appealing, and yet doomed to die. Depressed, I wake up.

The woman had no personal associations to the scene of the action. We can thus try to understand the canton of Glarus in itself. The Glarnerland region consists of mountains and valleys. It is known for a blend of industry and agriculture that is rich in tradition. So the dream is in a typical region of Switzerland, whose main characteristic is the successful combination of opposites. The beautiful stone house with the service buildings attached indicates a union of opposites namely an organic combination of living and working.

According to the dream, the dilapidated building with its still good fabric is dying. It has to give way to a building of international character, like the Sheraton chain, a uniform and soulless building. With a simple image, the dream shows how the creeping loss of identity is related to the increasing globalisation. The more such pleasing aspects as the high quality and the endearing features thus have to give way to a one-sided profit-mindedness thinking «of international character», the more any motivation to defend structures that have become so soulless is weakened. It is probably not by chance that in 1990 the cartoonist Raymond Burki linked the sale of

Fig. 18: Caricature by R. Burki on the takeover of the traditional Swiss company of Jacobs Suchard by the American cigarette company of Phillip Morris. Jacobs Suchard manufactures Toblerone chocolate, including the well-known triangle presented here as “tank barricade chocolate”. These were very common in Switzerland in the Second World War. Later, Jacobs Suchard was allocated to the globally active American company Kraft Food, and split off from Phillip Morris.

the traditional Swiss company Jacobs Suchard, which produced the famous chocolate Toblerone, to the international cigarette company Phillip Morris to a defeat of our national defence. There, too, economic reasons led to "the kiss" and the loss of independence.

You can generally see globalisation as an *ideology of delimitation*. The global activities of huge companies can largely escape democratic control and promote the uprooting of their senior staff. An increased awareness of this possibility of an outer and inner 'economic dictatorship' belongs to the sphere of the intellectual defence of the country. In this respect, the officer training of the Army would have an important task in duly relating these aspects of the *ethical responsibility* of the individual to the *res publica*. The militia thinking of Switzerland is based on this *polivalence of activities*.

Yet another dream on the Europe issue will be presented at the conclusion of this section, because it seems that Switzerland is considerably more problematic than generally supposed from the point of view of the unconscious. The dream comes from a Swiss pastor, in his mid-forties, who was not specifically concerned with political issues. On October 3, 1990, on the day of German reunification, he had a dream:

No. 36, Dream of the sanding over of Europe:

I see Europe from a bird's-eye view, uniform and colourless. Down in the south, the continent starts to break away. Italy in particular is in danger of being sanded over, i.e. crumbling down into the smallest particles and sinking. Only down in the far south is there still a rock island left. I think with horror of the billions of investments that are sinking or are needed for the rehabilitation. And also I think with horror of the huge underground weapons depot which I somehow know about. Some people commit suicide, by jumping into a raging torrent.

Of course, the chaplain who had this dream was happy about the reunification of Germany. But he was all the more scared by what he saw. As there was nothing threatening about the sanding over either for the dreamer internally or in his immediate vicinity, an interpretation of the dream as a personal matter made no sense. Spontaneously the dream was felt by the dreamer himself to be a warning about the widely acclaimed reunification of Germany, which was taking place on that day in the heart of Europe. Therefore, let us now examine what this dream might mean with regard to Europe.

At the beginning, all that the dreamer sees is the outline of Europe, uniform and colourless, that is to say united and with no differentiations. But then he sees that Europe begins to break away from the South, which means that the internal cohesion is fading. Instead of the billions calculated by the economists as a benefit of a united Europe, the dream says the exact opposite: the loss of large sums. Indeed, with most large-scale mergers, it has been proved that there only *seems* to be an improvement in overall profits. In Germany, for example, it was decided on economic grounds to merge smaller communities into larger units: In 1970 there were approximately 25'000 communities, and in 1980, there were around 8'500 large municipalities. But in the overall balance of this sensible 'new construction' there are also around 500'000 part-time, mostly volunteer, local politicians, who have become superfluous. Important links between citizens and State were thus rationalised away. This is an illustration of the social crumbling process that has been brought about by a one-sided rationalist concept of a merger. Today, with appalling clarity, we can deduce from the news from the South that billions of Euros are simply being squandered.

Where the European House, with the help of one-sided rational concepts, is built on sand, the collapse of Europe really does seem to be pre-programmed. This is something hardly anyone saw clearly at the time, in the euphoria of German reunification. The conclusion of the dream is:

I think with horror of the billions of investments that are going under or are needed for renovations. And also I think with horror of the huge underground weapons depot, which I somehow know about. Some people commit suicide by jumping into a raging river.

What then comes to light are huge weapons depots, i.e. a prepared potential aggressiveness of sinister proportions, which could plunge the West into a new dictatorship of war and misery. No wonder that in this vision, suicide seems to be the only way out for some.

The crumbling away of Europe starting in the south, led the dreamer to think of the Italian mafia. With regard to Europe's future, that will probably have something to do with the tendency found in all large organisations to more easily become corrupt, as a result of the lack of overview. The more political constructs become complex, the greater the feeling with the individual that his influence is insignificant anyway. He is just a cog in the machine. The reaction to this devaluation of individuals is an increasing selfishness, a personal maximisation of exploitation. This perception then becomes the dominant attitude. Seen in this way, the dream is a terrifying compensation of a generally too optimistic view of things in relation to the former steps towards a "new Europe". Today, over twenty years later, we must acknowledge that the dream image could actually prove to be true. Since then, the development in Europe has entailed a tremendous loss of energy. Converting this fatal dynamic into constructive energy could happen, if it were possible to understand what a real creative cultural revival in the West would mean. And so we strive to understand the symbolism of creative seeds from the unconscious, as specifically as was worked out in the chapter on the bridge into the future (page 83).

To sum up: the dreams listed in this chapter have given us clues about those unconscious drives which could threaten all of Europe as well as affecting the identity of Switzerland by undermining their powers of self-assertion. If the motivation for a United Europe is only a self-interested external search for the "Promised Land", thanks to which we will acquire even more prosperity and more freedom of movement, then Europe – judging from these dream images – will experience an impoverishment in mental biodiversity and consequently be robbed of its creative possibilities. But where the distinctiveness of individual units is overwhelmed by a materialistically-oriented collectivisation, a tremendous aggression accumulates in the unconscious. Unlived creative energy in an individual is usually transformed into destructive power. The sanding over and sinking of Europe into the sea would be the result of such soulless mergers. The unfortunately alarmingly clear-cut dream image would then mean psychologically that European culture could go under completely.

16. Rusty Switzerland

Now that we have examined the European environment of Switzerland from the perspective of the unconscious, let us return to the central problem of this country itself: why are so many people only too ready today to abandon the values of their own country to become part of the greater fabric of Europe? This question also troubled the Swiss man who was the source of the following dream. It gives us a deeper insight into the nature of the threat to our State system. The dream, slightly shortened here, occurred on January 2, 1991, at the beginning of the Jubilee year of the Confederation and a year before the vote for or against accession to the European Economic Area (EEA).

No 37, Dream about the rusty crate:

On a street in Jaipur in India I can see, in addition to other shrines, the shrine of the Black Madonna. It simply consists of a hole that goes from the side out onto the pavement. I ask myself: «Have people forgotten this place?» Now I am standing in front of this hole alongside a stranger and we are waiting in veneration of the Black Madonna. Then suddenly a fire salamander emerges from the hole. He moves onto the road and we must see to it that he will not be run over. So we place him in a large cardboard box that is there on the street. We put dry leaves in it to make him feel more comfortable. I'm pleased that we have managed to save the animal from being run over and that he lives, he exists.

Change of scene

I am listening to a lecture by Dr. X. He says in the lecture he had a dream in which he saw a large iron crate that was standing in the little river in Unterschächen and in it trout were living. Now I myself am experiencing the dream of Dr. X and see what he saw in the dream: the water could flow in and out of the crate even though it was closed and had no openings. And the fish were clearly content; they were inside the crate, but were also somehow able to get out. It was a good thing. But now the crate had been neglected and it was starting to rust. Unless something was done right away, the whole thing could fall apart. But this crate was Switzerland, he said. And then he went on to talk about the secret of the crate, including something about Beethoven's 7th Symphony.

The first part of the dream is set in India, where a shrine of the Black Madonna has fallen into oblivion. In Europe there are several shrines where a Black Madonna is revered, in Einsiedeln, Switzerland, for example, or Częstochowa in Poland. Such shrines have great popular appeal. Even today, here in Switzerland, many people, both young and old, go on pilgrimage to Einsiedeln, seeking aid and solace from the Black Madonna. When all else has failed, you still occasionally hear people say: «Go to Einsiedeln!» Where pointless suffering and confusion prevail, the Black Madonna, inexplicably, can somehow show that there is a meaning behind it all. As we know today, the shrines to the Black Madonna have enabled the ancient worship of the wisdom and healing power of the Goddess of Nature to survive.[77] But most people are unaware of this connection between the Black Madonna and the Goddess of Nature.

In the dream, there is now a shrine to the Black Madonna in India, in Jaipur, the capital of Rajasthan. In this Indian member state, 9 out of 10 inhabitants are Hindus and the remaining inhabitants are predominantly Muslims. There are virtually no Christians living there and so there is certainly no shrine to the Black Madonna in Jaipur. For the dreamer, a connoisseur of India, the country here in the dream represented a way of life far removed from that of us Europeans where, even today, Nature is publicly revered, famously made manifest in the attitude to the sacred cow. But according to the dream, even there, so far away, the shrine of the Black Madonna, which is a symbol of the Goddess of Nature, has sunk into oblivion.

Taking one's time, and approaching the shrine to Mother Nature with awe, leads to the appearance in the dream of the fire salamander. This animal, indigenous to Switzerland, is shiny black on top with bright yellow spots (Fig. 19). In the forest, these spots look like tiny lights, shining up at us from the dark ground. This is why the fire salamander has so often stirred people's imagination. For medieval Nature philosophers, this animal was a respected symbol of the *lumen naturae*, the light from the depth, the wisdom of Nature

77 Documentary evidence with F. Gustavson. *The Black Madonna*, Boston 1990.

Fig. 19: Fire salamander.

(See fig. 20). So we can interpret the appearance of the salamander as that mysterious and enlightening factor which reveals itself to Man from the shrine of the Goddess of Nature, far removed from today's collective consciousness. But for this to happen, he must take his time and wait in reverence to see whether the illuminating pictures or lights from the depths of the soul will appear.

Then the scene changes to a dream within the dream, as if it were an illustration or an insight into the nature of the fire salamander. It is a dream from Dr. X., folklorist and psychologist. His main preoccupation for many years has been to make folk-legends once again accessible to modern man by interpreting their symbols. This enables him to keep alive the knowledge of our ancestors in dealing with other-worldly powers. As an internal figure in the psyche of the dreamer, Dr. X embodies its ability to understand images symbolically, which is the vital bridge to knowledge from the depths, the *lumen naturae*, the wisdom of nature.

Fig. 20: Medieval representation of a fire salamander (from Michael Mayer, *Atalanta fugiens* 1618). Translation: "Like the salamander, the stone (of the philosophers) lives in the fire."

Only symbolic understanding opens up the path to those deeper insights that can reveal to us the illustrative knowledge inherent in Nature. For without this possibility to translate the illustrative language of the soul, enlightened consciousness would make nonsense of an image such as "Switzerland as an iron crate".

Then the dream continues further into the depths and the dreamer himself experiences the dream of Dr. X and sees the iron crate, which is Switzerland:

Now I myself am experiencing the dream of Dr. X and can see what he saw in the dream: the water could flow in and out of the crate even though it was closed and without any openings. And the fish were clearly content; they were inside the crate, but were somehow free to get out. And that was a good thing.

The symbolism of the iron takes us into the sphere of Mars, the ancient God of War. Even today, we use the phrases *iron will* and *iron discipline*, both characteristics of that God. A crate made of iron, which stands in water and which is closed and open at the same time, hints at the otherwise incomprehensible paradoxical mystery of our federalistic concept of State and its notion of freedom: Well-fortified, but solely to protect the vessel, withstanding current trends and yet open to new ideas, open to the world. It is a harmonious combination of demarcation and openness. The essence of the 700-year history of Switzerland is ultimately a secret that can probably not be explained rationally, a reconciling of such opposites that can only be perceived symbolically. The dream can thus be said to depict the essence of Switzerland.

The symbolism of the white Swiss cross against a red background is also an expression of the union of opposites. Bearing in mind the symbolism of the iron crate, in 1992, when the vote was held on whether or not to join the European Economic Area, it was probably right not to follow the urgent exhortation that we should jump onto the European Union train before it left. It corresponded rather to Swiss cautiousness to sit back and say: «Let the train go. We can always join later if it turns out to be a good thing.» So the iron crate would also be a symbol of Swiss doggedness.

Special mention is made in the dream of the fact that there are trout living in this iron crate. They seem to be quite content. They are inside the closed crate but paradoxically are *somehow free to get out*. Fish are not easy to grasp in water. Viewed on an internal psychic level, they correspond to the elusive contents of psychological depths. In his work *Aion*, C.G. Jung proved in great detail that fish often symbolise creative and redeeming fantasies.[78]

78 C.G. Jung. *Aion, Coll. Works* Vol.9.I, p. 103-172; §§ 162-266. (for example, the fish as Manu as a saviour, Christ the Redeemer as Ichtys = large fish etc).

The box with the salamander seems somehow to have a connection to the crate with the fish. In the first part of the dream, the salamander must be looked after and protected so that he is not killed by the traffic. We understood this act as a grasping of the *lumen naturae*, the wisdom of nature, so that these insights do not get lost in the hustle and bustle of everyday life. In the second part of the dream, trout are kept in the iron crate, but are not caught and killed. We could understand this aspect of the symbolism of Switzerland as follows: rather than following every whim of fashion, we remain firmly where we are so that the fish, the healing, creative fantasies, have a safe haven and can be grasped without being negatively affected. This shows that the "crate of Switzerland" is actually a protective framework, in which creative fantasies can live and thrive.

With its tolerance towards people who speak and think differently, Switzerland is actually a country that has always attracted – or produced – creative people. C.G. Jung is reputed to have once said that Switzerland is probably the only surviving natural park of the spirit, because the spirit in us is not uniform. This freedom is an optimal framework for creative work. Seen in this way, we can recognise in the symbol of this iron crate that there is something wonderful about the phenomenon known as Switzerland – something that cannot be defined with the simple logic of choosing between alternatives.

But now the crate had been neglected and it was starting to rust. Unless something was done right away, the whole thing could fall apart. But this crate was Switzerland, he said. And then he went on to talk about the secret of this crate, including something about Beethoven's 7th Symphony.

According to the dream, the iron crate is in an alarming state of neglect, which is why it has rusted. Iron is known to oxidise very easily, especially when it comes into contact with humid air. As dissolved oxygen is also found in water, iron can also corrode in water. According to the dream, therefore, the iron crate should not be neglected but must always be afforded protection against rust.

Now what might the symbolism of neglect mean? The opposite of neglect is interest, care and attention. In other words, what is lacking, according to the dream, is attention, conscious, loving care of the 'prison' called Switzerland. This striking image of Switzerland was used by Friedrich Dürrenmatt as a graphic representation of the paradoxical essence of Switzerland, by showing that inside 'the prison of Switzerland' the guards and the inmates are one and the same.[79] Interest in the iron crate of Switzerland would thus be an essential, rewarding and at the same time critical interest in our existing structures. As a result, newly emerging shortcomings can be exposed again and again and – if necessary – rectified and we shall increasingly be forced to listen to the views of others and, should the occasion arise, revise our own.

Apparently, the sense of loving care for the "crate of Switzerland" had ceased to be of great importance in the 1980s. It seems as if the sense of existence of this "Miracle Switzerland" had got lost for a substantial part of the population. If this is really the case, then our state system is regarded merely as a constricting prison, just as a 'marriage box' can become a prison unless it is constantly treated with loving affection as something meaningful, and thus prevented from falling into decay. The dream described the danger that Switzerland could be destroyed by rust as an acute one. From today's perspective, the rusty iron is an *alarmingly appropriate symbol of the corrosion of Swiss demarcation policy.*

At the end of the dream, Beethoven's Symphony No. 7 is mentioned. It seems to be an important aspect of the mystery of the iron crate. As we know from experience, the end of a dream indicates a possible solution to a problem that cropped up in the dream. This seems to be connected with polyphonic music by Beethoven. He wrote Symphony No. 7 in 1812, after having endured ten years of serious hearing difficulties which were to lead to total deafness in 1819. Beethoven's music here embodies something of both the tragic and the heroic, because the Symphony was composed despite fate having dealt him such a cruel blow. During the work on this Symphony, he was happy about the prospective defeat of Napoleon, and thus this Symphony is regarded as a consummate expression of Beethoven's desire for freedom. On the basis of these facts, we can now understand Symphony No. 7 as a means of preventing the disintegration of the iron crate. Music

79 F. Dürrenmatt, "Vaclav Havel in Zürich" in Bill Buford (ed.): *The Idea of Switzerland*, *GRANTA* 35, Spring 1991, p. 134. Translation of the speech entitled "Die Schweiz – ein Gefängnis" ("Switzerland – a prison") given by Friedrich Dürrenmatt on Vaclav Havel, on being awarded the Gottlieb-Duttweiler prize on November 22nd, 1990.

sets the mind in motion and is capable of creating a mood of connectedness. Probably, at the end of the day, only such a loving, feeling connection to Switzerland on the part of the individual can stave off one-sided disparaging criticism of this country. For if such criticism were to lead to neglect of the care of the miracle "crate of Switzerland", then the iron of the crate, i.e. the ability to demarcate and establish boundaries, would also soon be destroyed.

The following dream also picks up on the problem of cold feelings and the lack of love. It comes from a biology student who had attended my lecture at the ETH on "Archetypal dreams about environmental issues" in the summer of 1990. He wrote to me that after my lecture he had wished that he could have a "big dream" himself. On January 6, 1991, he had read in the news about the failure of the talks between the Foreign Ministers of the United States and Iraq. Afterwards the consequences of a possible Gulf war were shown. Among other things, a mock-up was shown which described the devastating consequences of war and the burning of the oil fields. The following night he wrote that for the first time he had had a dream which he felt did not just apply to him personally. This was his dream:

No. 38, Dream about masses of ice and soot:

With X I was riding in a train through a snow-covered landscape in Switzerland. The snow and the overcast sky were both a milky-cloudy colour. The train stopped in the middle of the countryside. X and I got out and set off to reach our destination on foot. But suddenly the clouds seemed to turn into lumps and became a mass of ice and soot, and this cloud mass descended upon us like a garage door being closed, and covered the whole area and all of us under a bell, and there was a dull sound as if stone slabs were being rubbed against each other. There was no contact with the outside world; nothing could be seen through the dirty curtain. Nothing could penetrate it. «This is the greenhouse effect,» I said, with great satisfaction, probably like the speculator when, contrary to all expectations, his forecasts prove to be accurate.

In fact, after the breakdown of talks between Secretaries of State Baker and Aziz, many people had the impression that the diplomatic channels were now permanently frozen. A Gulf war appeared inevitable. If the water of the emotional relationship with ice and soot freezes, then it is all over with human warmth, love and mutual understanding. People become hardened and look out only for themselves.

We are also familiar with the image of freezing from personal quarrels, when fronts harden. In such a state, one may also dream of winter freezing. In this dream, however, what the dreamer saw was mainly a suprapersonal aspect. He therefore went to the trouble of writing me a three-page letter. With C. G. Jung, too, we find this dream motif interpreted in the suprapersonal sense. In his memoirs, he describes how three times he had dreamed in the middle of summer that an Arctic coldness had descended, leaving the country frozen over. «I saw, for example, the whole of Lorraine and its canals frozen and the entire region totally deserted by human beings. All living green things were killed by frost. This dream came in April and May, and for the last time in June, 1914.»[80]

On August 1st, 1914 the First World War broke out. The dream image shows a symbolic view of the general glaciation of the climate, typical of wars, when man is hardened against his fellow-man.

At a time when general attention was focussed on events in the Gulf region, this dream speaks of a catastrophe that could take place in Switzerland, completely unexpectedly, so it seems. Soot, as dirt floating in the air, is a symbol of a dangerous intellectual pollution which impedes breathing and can cause cancer. The strange noise that is heard as if stone slabs are being rubbed together, points to a hardening of fronts, as one also says symbolically. Efforts to reconcile opposites are grated together as it were, which was the case in the unsuccessful attempts at mediation between Baker and Aziz.

The symbol of the greenhouse effect at the end of the dream is important. The so-called greenhouse problem occurs when there is an increase in carbon dioxide (CO_2) and trace gases in the atmosphere. This slows down even more the thermal radiation from the Earth's surface, causing a rise in temperature. Man is probably responsible for this since large amounts of CO_2 are being released by deforestation of tropical forests and the consumption of fossil fuels. He has long been aware that as a result, the global climate will

80 C. G Jung, *Memories, Dreams, Reflections*. New York 1961, 1965 (reprint), p. 176.

probably change and become warmer. This is in puzzling contrast to the freezing of the atmosphere, which is also the result of the greenhouse effect, according to the dream. But from a psychological point of view, overheating and freezing are not so far apart. For example, the Third Reich, with its warmongering fury and its intoxicating sense of victory, can be seen as a form of overheating. But at the same time it can also be seen as a freezing of emotions when we look at the diabolical cold-bloodedness with which dissidents were treated. In Dante's *Inferno*, freezing is to be found right at the bottom in Hell, the place which is also known for its unbearable heat. Both extremes are an intrinsic part of the inhuman-diabolical. Thus the end of the dream seems to be pointing in the following direction: talk of the external greenhouse effect is on everyone's lips today and is a recurring topic even with the experts. But hardly anyone seems to have realised that the mirror image to the external climate change might be an internal psychological greenhouse effect. This could be the effect of man's systematic isolation from cosmic connections and relatedness through our rationalistic world view. According to the dream, this could cause the climate of interpersonal relationships to suddenly freeze or overheat.

The worst surprises are usually those that are least expected. When all eyes are gazing outwards, which is where people expect the catastrophe to occur, it may well be that the real disaster comes from the inner psychological sphere. The history of the origins of the Third Reich should act as a warning to us that «there are instincts and archetypally driven attitudes of elemental strength which, against all expectations, against all reason, against all culture, can break out "overnight" [...]».[81]

In summary, the dream shows how a disaster announces itself, not only far away in the Gulf conflict (when Saddam Hussein did not voluntarily withdraw from Kuwait), but also shows that there could be something terrible lying in store for us in very close proximity. As long as it is just dreams of disasters, there is always the opportunity to shape the destructive energy of the unconscious in creatively constructive ways by becoming conscious of it. Therefore, as is highlighted in the dream at the end, it is important that

81 Translated from the sadly neglected book by Karl Schmid: *Europa zwischen Ideologie und Verwirklichung, Psychologische Aspekte der europäischen Integration,* Zurich 1966, p. 15.

these prophecies of doom be taken seriously, even if they run contrary to general expectations. It would be irresponsible self-delusion not to reckon with such destructive possibilities. But it would be an equally irresponsible act of fatalism not to reckon with the constructive potential of psychological powers. Vital pointers on how to understand the crisis and deal with it can be expected only from the unconscious background. The inner soul images reveal what is constellated in the collective unconscious.

17. Against the surrendering of identity: We need genuine visions

Any uncertainty in relation to Swiss independence must be addressed with appropriate measures. For the roots of the wish to surrender identity, as noted on page 140, are to be found outside the sphere of what can be grasped consciously or superficially. Wherever collective behaviour obeys irrational forces, we must find out, as has repeatedly been pointed out, about the unconscious drives. In dealing with the negative forces with which Switzerland has been faced for a long time, we need to acquire the necessary knowledge to understand the actual meaning of these trends. Only in this way can the constructive energy of the underlying archetype be supported.

On the subject of dealing with the forces that threaten to dissolve existing order structures, C. G. Jung had something fundamental to say: «The rising chaos demands new symbolic overall ideas, which include and express not only the existing systems, but also the essential content of the disorder. Such ideas would have a sort of magical effect because they banish the destructive forces of disorder, as has been the case for example in Christianity and all religions in general.»[82] «At any rate, we definitely need new visions», said the former State Councillor René Rhinow in a speech in 1991[83] and went on to add: «we must know (exactly) what we want, in order to unlock new energy, find new common ground, rediscover and restore old values, enriching them with new content against a changed background. We need to define "what makes sense" in the future, to use a popular phrase.» However justified this requirement is, we must nevertheless approach this task cautiously so as not to fall into the trap of thinking that *we ourselves* are capable of

82 C.G. Jung, *Letters II 1951-1961*, London 1975, p. 81.

83 Published in the *Neue Zürcher Zeitung* of the 12/13th January 1991 under 'Zeitfragen' (Contemporary questions), p. 21.

consciously creating visions. The basic models capable of creating new order out of chaos always had their roots in the unconscious. We have already seen such model dreams – the one about the mountain crystal and the one about attending to the iron crate. In dealing with these reports, other possible model dreams have come to me and they will be discussed later.

A man aged around 40, who was very preoccupied with Army matters, had the following dream on December 29th, 1990.

No. 39, Dream about the rose granite monolith:

I am together with the Army Head of training, Commanding officer Rolf Binder. The conversation revolves around the topic of willingness to defend one's country and the future of Switzerland. Somehow (a voice – God's voice?) we are told that the essential thing or the secret about this is a large reddish monolith of rose granite in Thalwil. Every soldier is given a little piece or has to go to Thalwil to collect it. That is then a rite of passage.

We now see the stone in front of us; it is huge. We are amazed that this was revealed to us so clearly. We then see how this stone is visited by young soldiers, but we also see that on no account must this be allowed to fall into oblivion.

The dream relates directly to the readiness to defend one's country and to the future of Switzerland and reveals in imagery the essential aspect of the country's willingness to do this. This is symbolised by a huge monolith of reddish rose granite. As a symbol is the best possible expression of facts that cannot be grasped on the conscious level, we have here an opportunity to find out more about what really lies at the heart of the Swiss motivation with regard to military and defence matters.

To fathom the meaning of this image of the monolith, we need to approach this symbol in the usual way: from various angles and with the necessary amplifications, in order to familiarise ourselves with it. The stone is made of granite. It is therefore first of all necessary for us to be clear about the nature of this type of rock. Granite is a plutonic rock, which arises through slow solidification of magma, usually at a depth of over 2000 metres, and is thus – in contrast to sedimentary rocks – not layered.

When magma from the Earth's interior cools down not too quickly, then parts made up of specific chemical composition are eliminated as crystals in a geometrically well-defined form in the transition of the aggregate liquid state into the solid mineral bodies themselves. The rocks thus formed by slow solidification therefore consist of several cohesive, adherent crystals, a grainy-looking crystal aggregate. The crystalline structure is very clearly formed, as with all plutonic rock, particularly with its main proponent, granite, (from the Latin word *granum* = grain). The granite is thus no amorphous mass, but a solid unit of various small, self-contained units, crystallised out in accordance with their own structural units. If we remind ourselves that the central mountains of Switzerland and also the lower lying subsoil of the central regions and of the Jura, the so-called bedrock, consist of such crystalline rock, we recognise in granite an amazingly true symbol of our State structure, which also represents a firmly established multifaceted unit.

Now the monolith is made of rose granite. We are not familiar with this type of reddish rock. But the dreamer knew rose granite from Aswan in Upper Egypt. This rock is extremely hard and tectonically has no faults. This meant that in Pharaonic Egypt, sarcophagi, statues and obelisks could be chiselled out without fear of cracks suddenly appearing in the rock. Since both the obelisk – especially with its small pyramid on the top – and the sarcophagus were a symbolic expression of the individual essence of soul and could not be destroyed by death, rose granite in Ancient Egypt is linked to Man's immortal personality centre (Fig. 21).

Since this association of the dreamer with rose granite takes us to Ancient Egypt, we should briefly remind ourselves of the essential features of this over 3'000-year-old Pharaonic culture. Probably the most important aspect of Pharaonic culture is that for the ancient Egyptians, death was not an absolute end. As long as a person had lived in accordance with the laws of Nature (*Ma'at*), he was assured of the transition to the experiencing of the eternal in Man; he became one of the blessed dead. The whole Pharaonic culture bears testimony to this elemental and innate belief in eternal life. Most of their creative powers by far were dedicated to the eternal and not to the temporal. It is hard to imagine Pharaonic culture without this belief in eternal life; it would certainly have been greatly impoverished.

In the later Hellenistic Egypt, the reddish or red stone as a symbol of the eternal in man lived on in Greek Alchemy and then, via Arabic and Latin

Fig. 21: Example of an Egyptian rose granite sarcophagus and obelisk.

Alchemy, became for us the famous symbol of the philosophers' stone. The production of this stone has nothing to do with the external making of gold, but represents a successful inner-spiritual union of opposites of the adept, and his integral strength as an individual.[84] Granite represents the unchanging and steadfast 'rock' of the established personality, and the pink colour stands for the invigorating effect on others radiated by people at one with themselves. With the philosophers' stone, a further distinctive characteristic is the mediation of meaning.

By way of an initial approach, let us now try to understand what this symbolic centre of our readiness to defend might mean. On the basis of the previous amplifications, we can regard the rose granite monolith as a symbol of the connecting indestructible essence of the "meaning and personality" of Switzerland. Judging from the dream, such a common centre does exist, but it is crucial that this knowledge should never be forgotten. Whoever finds this stone is, according to the dream, likely to be able to acquire and grasp – in the true sense of the word – these properties of pink granite, namely the mediation of meaning and the concept of the eternal. That would mean that he comes into contact with the meaningful and the eternal. Only this can cause a person to dedicate his life to freedom and independence. Without this personal *experience*, a person is only too ready to submit to those who are more powerful in the sense of "better red than dead". But beware! Here, too, we need to keep an eye on the two sides of the archetype, as the countless numbers of soldiers marching blindly into a 'hero's death' can testify. This experience could also be used to motivate soldiers to undertake objectives for the purpose of conquest and expansion. Only the will to defend freedom and independence and not pursue conquest and expansion can really connect with this symbolic centre of Switzerland. Switzerland's purely *defensive Army* is obliged to abide by this objective.

It must be assumed that nobody can convey any idea of this vital spiritual fact unless he himself has a piece of this rose granite in his pocket. Such a person can pass on knowledge of this centre by means of steadfast integrity and an appearance and attitude that inspire confidence. Ultimately the

84 Documentary evidence e.g. in *Muṣḥaf aṣ-ṣuwar;* Corpus Alchemicum Arabicum II.2. see red stone. Regarding the philosophers' stone, see manuscripts of Ostanes (1st century) in M. Berthelot *La Chimie du Moyen Age,* Paris 1898, Vol. III, p. 117.

motivating factor is the invigorating and stimulating charisma emanating from a leader at one with himself. The knock-on effect that such people have is common knowledge.

Now the large monolith in Thalwil, Switzerland, a commune on the left bank of Lake Zurich, comes up in the dream. The central stone of the Swiss military readiness to defend is thus not to be found in the heart of Switzerland on the Rütli meadow, not on the Gotthard or in the Federal Archives, but in a completely unexpected place, in Thalwil, which has not exactly played a prominent role in Swiss history. Since there is no such monolith in the outside world in Thalwil, we must try to shed light on the symbolic importance of this locality. The dreamer had two associations with Thalwil. As he grew up on the right-hand side of the lake, Thalwil was initially for him just somewhere "on the other side of the lake", on the left bank. That is the shadow side of the lake, and is thus, symbolically speaking, in the unconscious. His second association relates to an acquaintance who used to live there and at the time had problems with his inner world and the outside world, which gave him a sense of inferiority. Psychologically we could therefore look at the symbolism of Thalwil as follows: the secret of the Swiss willingness to defend its independence can be found in the unconscious, specifically *at the place of the feeling of inferiority*. In reality, the best way to consolidate oneself as a person is the willingness to confront one's shadow with one's own weak spot. "Only those who can laugh at themselves can be themselves" is a well-known truth. Those who do not really know their inferior sides and have not come to terms with them must always be trying to hide something. If, however, you are aware of your own weak spot, so to speak, you know that you are standing at the bottom and not at the top, so you cannot fall down. Paradoxically the insight into your own inferiority makes you feel calm and safe, because you can no longer be taken apart, as they say today. You have practically already taken yourself apart and therefore no longer feel the need to emotionally and aggressively take other people and other things apart.

There, in the place of inferiority or the "bone of contention", you will find, if you sit down and think about it, a connection to the secret of our acquiring the strength to become independent. This truth, according to the dream, must under no circumstances be lost: we must remain attentive in order not to lose sight of the location of our own inferiority. That is the strength of our direct democracy, that we have already had our inferior sides paraded before us in small groups by our opponents. If we Swiss are also collectively willing to deal with our typical Swiss bones of contention, for example, with our avarice, our role-model arrogance or our most hated enemies, we then acquire strength.[85] If this becomes a general attitude, then it is possible to exist even as a small country, and not humbly and self-guiltily bend the knee with every verbal attack on our separatism. This confrontation with one's own weak spots is always a union of opposites in the end. The philosophers' stone is a symbolic expression of this. We read in the dream:

Every soldier is given a little piece of the stone or has to go to Thalwil to collect it. This is like a rite of passage.

According to this man's dream, every single soldier gets a piece of this central stone; the personal connection to the rose granite appears here as their unifying symbol of Swiss military readiness to defend. On the other hand, in the dream of the young mother about the Repetition Course in (p. 107) we saw the Surikogi as the symbol of the individual readiness of women to offer resistance. This difference could be understood as an indication that there is a sensible allocation of duties between men and women with regard to the defence of Switzerland.

According to the dream, it is both a bringing and a fetching of the small piece of rose granite. It is not simply delivered to the soldier. Rather, according to the dream, it is like a rite of passage, an initiation into manhood, familiar to us from tribal cultures, where the elders connect young men to the Totem or the secret of the community, and where something must be acquired through accomplishment. Such an initiation is an *experience* which, according to the dream, must take place at some point in the life of the Swiss soldier.

But what does this rite of passage mean psychologically, and how can it be implemented? For this initiation in the dream, the soldier knocks out a small piece from the monolith. It calls for great strength, because the stone is so hard that this is possible only with a chisel and a hammer. As

85 In the Second World War, the military will to fight is said to have been encouraged by the Cabaret Cornichon, which pointed out the inferiority of the Swiss in an ironical, affectionate, humorous way.

the presence of the Army Head of Training is mentioned in the dream – there still was such a function at that time in the Swiss Army – we can interpret this motif as meaning that in Army training, but also in general, the *development of an independent and mature personality as a human objective* should once again become more of a focal point.

So much for an initial attempt at interpretation. The dream certainly has even more to reveal, but for the time being, we shall content ourselves with these outlines. In summary, the dream seems to be indicating that the decisive element in an assertion of Federal independence could easily sink into oblivion. This is namely a symbol of the union of opposites of stone and individuals: the one monolith, the rose granite, must connect with the individual soldier who has a piece of this reddish granite in his pocket. The union of opposites is passed on more generally in this way onto those individuals who are ready to accept the paradoxical truth of their own beings for what it is. They are then ready to see both their plus points and their negative points and face up to them. The individual must therefore himself actually be the repository of the thinking of the Swiss State, and be able to bear it within himself. This means that he must be able to accept what is different about himself, while learning that there is a meaning behind it. With the rose granite stone as the symbol of our willingness to take up arms, we acknowledge again the union of opposites as the quintessence of our nation; we have seen this also at national level in the open and closed iron crate, in the rock crystal and the Swiss flag.

The following dream comes from a Swiss who had been somewhat depressed the previous day, worrying about his country's future. On April 25, 1991, the year celebrating the 700th anniversary of the Swiss Confederation, he remembered the following excerpt from a long and extraordinarily impressive dream:

No. 40, Dream of a goddess with 4 red apples:

I see a goddess, depicted in the manner of the Egyptian goddesses. But on her head, instead of the usual attributes such as a Scorpion (Selkis) or a throne (Isis), she had four red apples. They were Bernese rose apples. […]

By way of reaction to the somewhat depressed mood of the dreamer on the previous day about the future of Switzerland, the only thing that he was able to retain from the long dream was this image. That might generally be understood as: Just look at that.

As was the case with the dream about the rose granite monolith in Thalwil, in this dream fragment, too, the distant past of Pharaonic Egypt is linked with something basically Swiss, for Bernese rose apples are an old, typically local variety of apple, and the word 'Bern' in the name refers to Switzerland's capital. Here again, we must seek to understand the vision of this goddess with the aid of amplifications.

Any representation of Pharaonic deities is distinctive, in that the essence of a deity is represented with her central symbol on her head. The essence of the goddess Selkis, who brings illness but also heals, would therefore be the scorpion. The essence of the goddess Isis, the mother of Horus, the first Pharaoh, would be the throne (Fig. 22). Now in this dream, we see a goddess with a typical Swiss attribute, namely the four local red apples. We in the Christian West have had no goddesses for a long time. But in Switzerland, we have known Helvetia since the 17th century.[86] With the growing national consciousness in the 19th century and the founding of the Swiss Federal State in 1848, Helvetia gained in importance. She appeared on coins and stamps, and in political and patriotic representations. There is a portrait of Helvetia on Swiss coins and her name is on Swiss postage stamps. This female figure symbolises the emotional *feeling of togetherness* of Switzerland, complementary to the juridical togetherness based on reason. If we in Switzerland could speak of an indigenous binding force, then it would probably be Helvetia. The fact that the goddess has four Bernese rose apples on her head links her to Switzerland.

Now this dream image could be understood as saying that the Swiss Helvetia has a new symbol on her head. Maybe that is why the dream creates a connection between the typical Swiss fruit and an Egyptian representation of a goddess, for a distinctive feature of Pharaonic culture is its differentiated

86 1672 Johann Caspar Walker staged his play "Eydtgenossisch Contrafeth Auff- und Abnemmender Jungfrawen Helvetiae" and created a new identification figure for the unity of the Swiss Confederation at a time when there were interdenominational disputes. (Georg Kreis, "Helvetia", in: *Historisches Lexikon der Schweiz*.)

Fig. 22: Pharaonic goddesses: on the left, the goddess Isis, with the throne on her head, and on the right, the goddess Selkis, with the scorpion on her head.

knowledge of other-worldly powers. With this knowledge, the ancient Egyptians were always anxious to constantly renew the essence of their symbols and keep the experience of them alive. For they sensed that the power of symbols wanes and that the link to the unifying other-worldly powers could thus get lost. Helvetia, too, the symbol of the Swiss feeling of togetherness, is less powerful so that according to the dream, a renewal or extension of its symbolism has become necessary.

But what do the four red Bernese apples mean? Like all fruit, apples are "children" of their trees and plants and so belong to the maternal and hence the feminine principle. We are familiar with the apple as a symbol from the Christian creation myth. There it symbolises knowledge of good and evil, for that is what the serpent promised Eve if she ate of the forbidden apple.

Fig. 23: Helvetia, exhausted by the journey, having laid down her shield and sword. Sculpture by the Swiss artist Bettina Eichin on the Kleinbasle bridgehead of the Basle middle bridge.

So it has to do with the ability to make moral distinctions. In Switzerland, of course, the apple on the head of William Tell's son is a famous symbol of the aim of the fearless freedom fighter. As a round sphere, the apple was also a symbol of wholeness, one example being in the form of the imperial apple. If a motif appears in fours it usually indicates a content that can be recognised from all sides.[87] So if Helvetia is to be extended by the symbolism of the four apples, it expresses something about the essence of the soul of Switzerland, as is the case with the four sides of the Swiss cross.

What the goddess wears on her head symbolises her highest goal, that for which she strives. The throne on the head of Isis symbolises the desire of the goddess to be a base for the Pharaoh, just as the crown of the King or the tiara of the Pope symbolise their aim to reconcile the opposites of the

87 Documentary evidence Th. Abt, *Introduction to Picture Interpretation*, Zurich 2005.

Empire or of the Church. The goal of the goddess with four Bernese rose apples on her head, the Helvetia, would be a more differentiated, conscious Eros – understood in the broader sense as a connecting principle (Fig. 24). That would be an awareness of what Karl Schmid called the "Federal disposition". One can see them, as he further wrote, «not as a kind of 'Neutrality', both towards Unitarianism and towards Pluralism, but as something that stems from the adopting of a firm moral position.» And he goes on to say: «We can only speak of federalistic feeling if the two antagonistic tendencies are *conscious and consciously approved.*»[88] Only from this deliberately sustained field of tension can a renewed sense of connection, a new awareness of the value of Switzerland, be born.

Fig. 24: Four Bernese rose apples, as in the dream image of the Goddess with the four Bernese rose apples on her head.

88 Karl Schmid, *Europa zwischen Ideologie und Verwirklichung*, Zurich 1966, p. 137 (Accentuation by Th. Author).

The dreams and their interpretations presented here are first impulses from the unconscious concerning the question of the renewal of visions which we need in our country. If we continue to work on a relationship with this root sphere – this is my belief – we can hope to take countermeasures against the danger of surrendering the identity of a federalist Confederation that has evolved over centuries.

18. Epilogue

The dream collection of Charlotte Beradt – from the period 1933-1939 – is evidence of a seemingly magical force that was able to cast its spell over the German people in the era of National Socialism. In the dreams presented here, Hitler and his henchmen are in possession of seemingly inexplicable magic powers. As we saw, for example, in the «Dream about the treacherous stove» (page 24), matter that was apparently dead for modern Man came alive in dreams during the Nazi regime and, as if in alliance, so to speak, with the reign of terror, seemed to consolidate it mysteriously from within. We saw a correlation with the fact that matter rejected by Christianity was left to the Devil, the Lord of this world. In dreams like this from Beradt's collection, it seems as if matter had avenged itself for the fact that it *was no longer accorded the divine quality and thus the veneration* to which it was entitled in non-patriarchal religions.

The counterpart to the Christian God image, the opposite of the "loving God" is the Devil, the Lord of this world. In Germany, this figure bore the characteristics of Wotan, the Germanic, one-eyed storm God and bringer of culture, who had been ousted in the enforced Christianisation of Germany by Charlemagne. In the Nazi era, this one-eyed storm God was able to gain the upper hand over the Christian God and lash out at will. This archetypal force, coming both from without and also – by way of the unconscious – from within, suddenly and unexpectedly robbed the Germans of the freedom of individual consciousness. In the 1930s, with devilishly seductive phrases, the word of God, the word of the loving, all-gracious God, was turned into the opposite, and a whole civilised nation literally went out of its mind.

The horrors of the First World War had already shaken to its very foundations the Christian belief in a caring, all-gracious God. Later, there was the economic depression of the early 1930s, with the enormous problem of unemployment. In Germany, it looked as though this could no longer be solved on the basis of the then Constitution. After the humiliating defeat in the First World War, this led to a great yearning for economic revival, restoration of order and a renewed sense of self-worth. It was against the background of this desperate situation that someone – Hitler – came along and volunteered to "take over responsibility and bring you the salvation, order and honour you long for. "With such promises as these, the way was paved for the seizing of power by the opponents of a no longer credible" loving God", and consequently for the diabolical conformity known as *Gleichschaltung* and State slavery, as illustrated so vividly in the dreams collected by Beradt.

If we look back at this new dream collection, compiled some fifty years later, we can also detect indications of the working of an unconscious driving force which was once again able to tyrannise the people. Let us take as an example the «Dream of the amusement park with a thermostat» (p. 48). In this dream, too, there is an apparently magical force – creating its effect in the *power of the words and slogans* of the thermostat, which leads the people in the amusement park to pursue a definite course of action – quite similar to the power of the Nazi propaganda of the 1930s. Here, too, there are words derived from matter – this time delivered by a sinister apparatus – which tyrannise people under the plastic or glass bell in an uncontrollable way. In this dream, it is also as if matter had come alive in order to carry out devilish acts, so that an uncontrolled dynamism prevails in the amusement park. The invisible 'programmer' of the mysterious thermostat in this dream shows traits comparable to the matter that came alive in Beradt's dream collection. This shows that the magically effective force which at that time led to the Nazi dictatorship is still alive, in a position to trigger off at any time an avalanche of joyfully ecstatic enthusiasm but also passionately diabolical obsession. In this 'programmer' acting in the background of the consumer park, *Wotan reveals himself in altered form.* This is no longer the aggressive storm God. Today, this archetype is seen as *a peace-loving destroyer of separation and demarcation.* With sweet-talk assurances of economic growth, peace and unbounded freedom, a better world is promised. This dynamic – understandable after the horrors of two world wars – has Europe under its spell. The result is that not a few people once again see 'Forward' and only 'Forward' as the path to the future, even if the idea can no longer be dismissed that this step might turn out to be a false one. It seems as if there is no stopping this sinister momentum which is being activated in the background of this day and age.

The remarkable thing about our dream collection is that two of the dreams that seemed to be particularly threatening occurred when the dreamer in question had been informed about new prospects for peace. The «Dream about the amusement park with thermostat» occurred in 1989, the day before the signing of the general nuclear disarmament treaty by the major powers, giving rise to great hopes for peace after the Cold War. And the «Dream about the sanding over of Europe» (p. 151) is also very disturbing. It also occurred in 1989, following the enthusiastically acclaimed reunification of Germany. In this dream, the dreamer looks on as Europe breaks away from the South and slowly sinks into the sea. If, today, over twenty years later, we look at the crisis-ridden Mediterranean countries of Europe, this dream seems to be a sombre premonition of a potential disaster. Let us recall how the dream ends: *I think with horror of the billions of investments that are sinking or are needed for the rehabilitation. And also I think with horror of the huge underground weapons depot which I somehow know about. Some people commit suicide by jumping into a raging torrent. The vast potential for aggression referred to here even drives some individuals who have lost all hope to commit suicide.*

As we have seen, each archetype can, on the one hand, make people obsessed and blind, and, on the other hand, can have an edifying and thus meaningful effect. For example, the «Dream about the bridge to the future» (page 83) showed how the images from the unconscious background of the psyche, symbolised as a grandfather or "spirit of the ancestors", can convey something constructive and meaningful to the "old men of the future". In this dream, thanks to the symbol of the bridge, the dynamic from the unconscious is seen as positive energy *created by the dream itself.* And for example, in the «Dream of the goddess with four Bernese rose apples on her head» (page 173), the symbol-forming power of this unconscious spirit created a new enlivening and invigorating symbol. This dream image of a divine Helvetia is an extended and thereby renewed symbol of the emotional, inner spiritual cohesion of Switzerland.

From the experience of the history of mankind, and many years of research into depth psychology, we know that these big dreams can have a meaning not only for the individual dreamers themselves, but also for the collective. Such dreams depict what might be destructive in people's unconscious psychological background but also what could be of cultural benefit. If it is possible to 'incubate' such archetypal dream pictures with the necessary care and attention, the dangerous tendencies that they contain can be recognised, registered, understood and hence transformed. Their destructive tendency can thus be averted. And the uplifting and edifying images that emerge from this dark unconscious background can act as a bridge to a future worth living.

Charlotte Beradt collected the dreams only after Hitler came to power. Thus the possible insights which might have been gained from these dream images had no influence on contemporary events. Almost without exception, the dreams ended on a note of despair. Her dream collection remains valuable as a *salutary warning to future generations*, particularly – it should be stressed again – by showing that the imagery from the subconscious mind can convey an idea of what is being activated in the psychological background.

***

On the basis of the newer dream collection presented here, an investigation was conducted in parts II to IV into what is constellated in the suprapersonal unconscious background. For according to many of the dreams, a strong wind is blowing again today, and not just over Europe. It is uprooting countless numbers of people, as well as sweeping aside established structures and boundaries. At the end of Part I, a question was posed, the gist of which was: given this dynamic, does clinging to tradition-based, tried and tested structures mean more of a "regressive isolation", or does resistance to such processes of disintegration call for the exercising of self-restraint to ensure a better future? Or is there perhaps a need today for a totally *new perspective* if society is to develop in a positive way?

We have looked at the picture material from the unconscious and raised questions about its meaning. According to these dreams, if there is to be any sustainable development in society, it will probably be crucial whether individual people succeed in avoiding the possessive, demonic energy of the activated fascination exerted by matter and instead encounter this *feminine life principle (which corresponds to the Chinese yin) with an attitude that is both respectful and questioning, thus providing support for its creative and cultural side*. For this, it is necessary to be able to cope with the above-mentioned tension of opposites between the value of adherence to the tried and trusted and the necessary urge to move forward, enabling something new, the *symbolic third*, to manifest itself. What is apparent from the experience of depth psychology is that the conscious dealing with such a tension of opposites by the individual leads to the possibility of the birth of new symbols that are future-oriented and constructive. However, the next step, namely the *grasping and incorporating of these symbols into everyday life*, is of crucial importance.

Speaking in the imagery of the «Dream of the water samples» (p. 39), we need the healing water from the lake on which Europe floats. The healing aspect of this water – in which we have recognised a symbol of the unconscious – is the spirit contained therein. This spirit is to be found in the initially incomprehensible images which greet us as they rise up from the depths of the psyche. As stated in the introduction, and now illustrated in dream documents, dreams also provide orientation in the external world if they are incubated carefully and critically. When dreams relate to collective questions in the outside world, they can also – and this is now my repeatedly confirmed hypothesis – be of importance for society as a whole. It is in these dream images that we see the workings of *a spirit of matter or nature*. There is a surprising intelligence at play which determines the symbolic processes of our dreams. This is why, as stated earlier, these images are able to capture the dangerous and powerful Wotanic dynamic drive that appears today in changed form, thus enabling it to reveal a side that is both meaningful and edifying.

As can be determined empirically on the basis of numerous other "big dreams", as well as in this dream collection, a valley, a region, a nation, as well as an individual, can have a *distinctive sense of uniqueness*, that is to say, can be experienced with a kind of 'personality character'. In the specific case of this collection, various dreams about Switzerland have conveyed such an impression of uniqueness and independence. A case in point would be the «Dream about the Gotthard crystal.

Other dreams, such as the «Dream about the courageous woman of Zurich» (p. 73), or the «Dream about the Repetition Course for women» (p. 107), clearly reveal the importance attached to the defence of the Swiss State system. This can be seen and summed up in the *relationship of trust* that the Swiss have with their State, a State in which the electorate has the last word. The Swiss political system is characterised by a unique, confederated, small-scale organisation, direct democracy and the principle of the militia system. The two last-mentioned signify that not only political duties, but also national defence are largely carried out by the citizens themselves. A wide range of activities thus become a civic duty. The result is that quite a large number of people have the opportunity, however briefly, to take part in the decision-making process, to bear their share of responsibility and thereby acquire an appreciation of what it means to be member of a democratic society. Finding time to be involved in such activities is the price to be paid for freedom.

On the political level, this means that discussions and arguments with political opponents can take place in freedom in each municipality, in each canton, as well at federal level. In this way, any politician will have his own one-sidedness and weaknesses paraded before him by his opponents. A sort of "verbal warfare" is constantly being waged. In a direct democracy, there is room for different and conflicting views and personalities That is essential if there is to be any fruitful interplay of opposites. Thus in a direct democracy, nobody can carry on too long without acknowledging his or her shadow.

However, this type of direct democracy works only as long as the individual is always prepared to maintain a critical distance from his own opinion. But if people claim to be totally convinced of what is right and what is wrong, then they lose contact with their own doubts. This is always the beginning of a one-sidedness, a one-eyed view, one might say. In time, this can degenerate into a kind of 'dictatorship' within the individual, because as a result, one's own doubts are increasingly glossed over with a fanatical zeal, and *dangerously authoritarian fascism* is transferred to – and *only seen in – the other party*. By way of suggestibility, this one-sided view of things can spread over the masses, as was the case in the 1930s, at the time of the advent of the Nazi regime. Therefore, any correction to the individual must start with questions such as: where and when am I irrevocably stuck with a cut-and-dried opinion? Where and why do I become uncontrollably emotional? Why do I see the devil in the enemy? The more stubbornly I insist that I am in the right, the more fanatically and one-sidedly obsessed I become. I then tend to form an opinion – to be more precise – a prejudice about my opponent that I absolutely refuse to change.

Direct democracy thrives on meeting and discussing with people who may have different views. However, where the individual is swept along by the crowd and lapses into an attitude of indifferent, could-not-care-less irresponsibility and passive acceptance of State paternalism, this opportunity, and hence the possibility for self-correction, disappears. It is therefore necessary first and foremost to defend the *autonomy and freedom of the individual*, but also the *viability of small units*, in all places and at all times. This for me is the profound, central message behind the dream collection edited in this book.

Part V

Appendix

1. Bibliography

Abt, Theodor: *Entwicklungsplanung ohne Seele?* Sozio-ökonomische und psychologische Aspekte der Entwicklungsplanung im Berggebiet, Dissertation ETH Zurich, Bern and Frankfurt am Main 1977.

- "Planning without Shadow". In: *The Archetype of Shadow in a Split World*. International Congress of Analytical Psychology Berlin, September 2, 1986. p. 91-110.

- *Progress without Loss of Soul.* Toward a wholistic approach to modernization planning. Wilmette, Ill. 1989.

- "Forschung am Wendepunkt. Zur Praxis des ganzheitlichen Denkens". In: *Landwirtschaft Schweiz*; vol. 3/5 (1990); p. 259–265.

- "Auf der Suche nach einem Dialog mit der Natur". In: *GAIA, Ökologische Perspektiven für Wissenschaft und Gesellschaft*, I/6 (1992), S. 318-332.

- "Archetypische Träume zur Beziehung zwischen Psyche und Materie". In: H. Atmanspacher, H. Primas and E. Wertenschlag-Birkhäuser (Eds.): *Der Pauli-Jung-Dialog und seine Bedeutung für die moderne Wissenschaft.* Berlin 1995, p. 109-136.

- *Introduction to Picture Interpretation*, Zurich 2005.

- *Wissen und Ahnung. Landentwicklung mit Seelengewinn.* Niederalteich 2007.

Attenhofer, Elsie: *Réserve du Patron. Im Gespräch mit K.*, Stäfa, 1989.

Beradt, Charlotte: *The Third Reich of Dreams*. Transl. from the German by Adriane Gottwal; With an essay by Bruno Bettelheim. Chicago 1968.

Berthelot, Marcellin: *La Chimie du Moyen Age*, vol. III, Paris 1898.

Bible: *The New Cambridge Paragraph Bible*, with the Apocrypha, King James Version, ed. by David Norton. Cambridge (Eng.) 2005.

Bonjour, Edgar: *Geschichte der schweizerischen Neutralität. Vier Jahrhunderte eidgenössischer Aussenpolitik,* vols. 4-9, Basle, Stuttgart 1971-1976.

Brücker, Josef: *Ansprache* von alt-Landammann Josef Brücker anlässlich der Diamantfeier vom 2. September 1989 in Altdorf, photocopied.

Corpus Alchemicum Arabicum, edited by Th. Abt and W. Madelung. Zurich 2001f.

Damals. Das Magazin für Geschichte, No 44/2 (2012). "Die SS. Macht des Schreckens". Leinfelden-Echterdingen 2012.

Dändliker, Karl: *Geschichte der Stadt Zürich,* Band 1. Zurich 1908.

Dürrenmatt, Friedrich: "Vaclav Havel in Zürich" in: *The idea of Switzerland,* edited by Bill Buford, *GRANTA* 35, Spring 1991. p. 126-144.

Edward, Betty: *Drawing on the Right Side of the Brain*, Los Angeles 1979, London 1981.

Eusebius von Caesarea: *Life of Constantine*. Introduction, translation and comment by Averil Cameron and Stuart G. Hall. Clarendon ancient history series. Oxford 1999.

Franz, M.-L. von: *Creation myths*. New revised edition, Boston 1995. First edition: *Patterns of Creativity mirrored in Creation Myths.* Zurich 1972.

- *On Divination and Synchronicity. The Psychology of meaningful Chance.* Studies in Jungian psychology by Jungian analysts 3, *Toronto 1980.* For the quoted foreword, newly inserted in the German version: *Wissen aus der Tiefe, Über Orakel und Synchronizität*, Munich 1987.

- *Number and Time: Reflections Leading Toward a Unification of Depth Psychology and Physics.* Evanston, Ill. Northwestern University Press 1986.

Freud, Sigmund: "Letter to A. Einstein", September 1932. In chapter: "Why War?", in: *The Standard Edition of the Complete Psychological Works of Sigmund Freud.* Translated from the German under the general editorship of James Strachey in collaboration with Anna Freud.

Assisted by Alix Strachey and Alan Tyson. London 1964, reprint 1978, vol. 22, p. 199-215.

Gennep, Arnold van: *The rites of passage*. Transl. by Monika B. Vizedom , Introduction by Solon T. Kimball, London 1960, reprint as part of Religion, rites & ceremonies vol. 3, 2004. French Original: *Les Rites de passage,* Paris 1909.

Giger, Hans: *Die verlorene Ehre der Mutter Helvetia. Politische Machtentfaltung im Fokus allgemeiner Rechtsprinzipien*, Zurich 2012.

Goethe, Johann Wolfgang von: *Gedichte 1756-1799.* Collection of all works, letters, diaries and interviews. Section I, vol. 1. Edited by Karl Eibl, Frankfurt 1987

Goodall, Jane: *Reason for Hope. A spiritual journey.* New York 1999.

Grzimek, Bernhard: *Grzimek's Animal Life Encyclopedia*. Vol 16. Series edited by Michael Hutchins (series editor), Melissa C. McDade, (vol. 12-17). Detroit 2001-2004^{2}.

Gustafson, Fred: *The Black Madonna*. Boston 1990.

Hofstadter, D.R.: *Gödel, Escher, Bach. An eternal golden braid.* New York 1979.

Huber, Martin: "Ironie der Geschichte: Das AJZ wurde zum Polizeimuseum." In: *Tagesanzeiger*, September 9, 2011.

The I Ching or Book of Changes. Bollingen Series 19. The Richard Wilhelm translation rendered into English by Cary F. Baynes. Foreword by C.G. Jung. New York 1952.

Isler, Godhilf: *Lumen naturae,* Egg 2000.

- *Die Sennenpuppe, Eine Untersuchung über die religiöse Funktion von einigen Alpensagen,* Schriften der schweizer Gesellschaft für Volkskunde vol. 52, Basle 1971.

Jung, Carl Gustav: "Aion. Researches into the Phenomenology of the Self', *Collected Works* 9/II. New York 1959.

Jung, Carl Gustav: *Letters Vol 2: 1951-1961*. Selected and edited by Gerhard Alder in collaboration with Aniela Jaffé. London 1975.

- *Memories, Dreams, Reflections*. New York 1962.

- *Mysterium Conjunctionis. An Inquiry into the Separation and Synthesis of Psychic Opposites in Alchemy*, *Collected Works* 14, New York 1963, Princeton, New Jersey 1970^{2}.

- "Wotan", in *Collected Works* 10. Princeton New Jersey, 1964, p. 371-99.

Koran, see Qur'an

Kreis, Georg: "Helvetia", in: *Historisches Lexikon der Schweiz in 13 Bänden,* vol. 6, Basle 2007.

Ladwig-Winters, Simone: *Anwalt ohne Recht - Das Schicksal jüdischer Rechtsanwälte in Berlin nach 1933*, edited by Bundesrechtsanwaltskammer in Berlin, Berlin 2007.

Looser, S.: "Überlebt die Schweizer Armee?" in: *Intra, Zeitschrift für Psychologie in der Gesellschaft,* Number 1, Oktober 1989.

Müller-Herold, Ulrich: "Liquidum incognitum: [unbekanntes] flüssiges Wasser", in: *Schweizerische Monatshefte*, No. 11 (2007), p. 35-36.

Matter, Martin: *P-26. Die Geheimarmee, die keine war*, Baden 2012.

Mylius, Johann Daniel: *Philosophia reformata continens libros binos*, Frankfurt am Main 1622.

Narveson, Jan: "Is Pacifism Self-Refuting?" in: Bleisch, Barbara; Jean-Daniel Strub (Eds.): *Pazifismus. Ideengeschichte, Theorie und Praxis*. Bern 2006.

Orwell, George: *Nineteen Eighty-Four.* London 1949.

Pestalozzi, Johann Heinrich: "Ideen." In ders.: *Sämtliche Werke. Kritische Ausgabe.* Edited by Artur Buchenau, Eduard Spranger, Hans Stettbacher. Berlin and Zurich 1927–1996.

Picard, Max: *Hitler in uns selbst,* Erlenbach-Zurich 1946.

Qur'ān, The Holy: English translation of the Meanings and commentary. Revised and Edited by The Presidency of Islamic Researchers (IFTA) ; Riyad, 1410 H.

Renner, Eduard: *Goldener Ring über Uri: ein Buch vom Erleben und Denken unserer Bergler, von Magie und Geistern und von den ersten und letzten Dingen.* Zurich 1941. New edition 1991.

Rhinow, René: "Braucht die Schweiz Visionen?". Revised and shortened version of a presentation given at a general meeting of "Agir pour demain" at 4th of December 1991 in Bern. *Neue Zürcher Zeitung (NZZ)*, January 12/13, 1991, Zeitfragen, ...

Schiller, Friedrich: *William Tell,* translated from the German in the metre of the original by Theodore Martin; illustrated by Rafaello Busoni. New York 1952.

Schmid, Karl: *Europa zwischen Ideologie und Verwirklichung*, Psychologische Aspekte der europäischen Integration, Zurich 1966. New edition: Stäfa and Schaffhausen 1990.

Šimek, Rudolf: *Die Edda.* Munich 2007.

Somm, Markus: *General Guisan. Widerstand nach Schweizerart,* Bern 2010.

Walder, Ernst: "Stanser Verkommnis*", in: Historisches Lexikon der Schweiz in 13 Bänden,* vol. 11, Basle 2012.

Wisnewsky, Gerhard: *Verheimlicht, vertuscht, vergessen. Was 2011 nicht in der Zeitung stand*, Munich 2012.

Zamiatin, Yevgeny (Eugene Ivanovich): *We.* New York 2012 (reprint). First english edition 1959.

Zosimos von Panopolis: *Muṣḥaf aṣ-ṣuwar*. (The Book of Pictures), english translation by Salwa Fuad and Theodor Abt. In: Corpus Alchemicum Arabicum II.2 (CALA II.2), Zurich 2011.

2. List of dreams

Part I

Part II

Part III

Part IV

3. List of illustrations

If sources are not mentioned, the author of the illustration could not be identified.

Fig. 1: Formation of SS-Unit „Adolf Hitler". In: *Damals. Das Magazin für Geschichte*, 44/2 (2012), p. 17.

Fig. 2 : Lawyer Dr. M.Siegel with placard. In: Bundesrechtsanwaltskammer (Hg.): *Anwalt ohne Recht. Schicksale jüdischer Anwälte in Deutschland nach 1933*. be.bra verlag Berlin, 2007, p. 30.

Fig. 3: Roll-call in the Sachsenhausen concentration camp. In: *Damals. Das Magazin für Geschichte,* 44/2 (2012), p.15.

Fig. 4: Brown June Beetle (*Philopertha horticola)*. By Holger Gröschl.

Fig. 5: Scarab beetle with ball.

Fig. 6: Egyptian scarab. Tomb of Ramses VI, Theben Mapping Project (Kent Weeks).

Fig. 7: Wotan, the one-eyed wanderer. Picture of the Swedish painter Georg von Rosen (1843-1923)

Fig. 8: Fountain with the courageous Zurich woman the Lindenhof in Zurich. By Theodor Abt.

Fig. 9: Courageous Zurich woman. Close-up detail of fig. 8.

Fig. 10: Rütli Report of July 25, 1950. From: Markus Somm, *General Guisan*.

Fig. 11: Japanese Surikogi (sketch). By Theodor Abt.

Fig. 12-13:Illustration of the dream about the Gotthard crystal and about Swiss cantons with keys. Sketch done by dreamer.

Fig. 14: Giant crystal. By Franz von Arx.

Fig. 15: Wooden well trough. By Patrick Bürgler.

Fig. 16: Prayer call of the herdsman. Innerrhoden, 1900. By Cyrill Schläpfer.

Fig. 17: Beaver construction. Source of photography unknown.

Fig. 18: Caricature on the takeover of Jacobs Suchard by Philllip Morris. By R. Burki.

Fig. 19: Fire Salamander. Photography by B. Trapp in: Marc Staniszewski: *Salamander und Molche Europas, Nordafrikas und Westasiens*. Frankfurt 2011, p. 121.

Fig. 20: Salamander in the fire (medieval representation). Michael Maier, *Atalanta Fugiens,* 1618. Emblema XXIX, p. 405.

Fig. 21: Above: Egyptian rose granite sarcophagus. Theben Mappig Project (Kent Weeks).
Below: Rose granite obelisk. By Antonio Attini in: David Roberts; Fabio Bourbon, Antionio Attini: *Egypt. Yesterday and Today Egypt.* Lithographs and Diaries by David Roberts, Text by Fabio Bourbon. Photographs by Antonio Attini. Cairo 1996, p. 262.

Fig. 22: Pharaonic goddesses Isis and Selkis. From the tombs of the valley of Queens; right side: From the tomb of Queen Nefertari.

Fig. 23: Tired Helvetia. Sculpture by Bettina Eichin on the Middle Bridge of Basle, Kleinbasel.

Fig. 24: Bernese rose apples. By Götz Eble for "Müller Lebensraum Garten" company.

4. Index

– D –

– W –

– Y / Z –